Twelve Steps to Spiritual Wholeness

A Christian Pathway

Philip St. Romain

LIGUORI
PUBLICATIONS

One Liguori Drive
Liguori, MO 63057-9999
(314) 464-2500

ISBN 0-89243-429-5
Library of Congress Catalog Card Number: 91-77986

Copyright © 1992, Liguori Publications
Printed in U.S.A.

Cover design by Pam Hummelsheim

Contents

Introduction

My first book for Liguori Publications, *Becoming a New Person: Twelve Steps to Christian Growth,* was published in 1984. As far as I know, it was the first book that adapted the Twelve Steps to a specifically Christian spirituality.

Since then, I have gone on to publish other books with Liguori, and a plethora of works on the Twelve Steps — many from a Christian viewpoint — have appeared. It would be an understatement to say that the Twelve Steps have "caught on."

When the editors of *Liguorian* magazine approached me about writing a yearlong series of articles on the "Twelve Steps of Spirituality," I was not surprised that they chose this topic. I was surprised, however, that they were asking *me* to write these articles. My initial response was to suggest that they serialize *Becoming a New Person.* But Father Allan Weinert, the editor-in-chief, would hear nothing of this. He challenged me to think of a way to develop the Steps without focusing specifically on recovery from addiction and without merely rehashing my earlier book.

After some thought, I concluded that I indeed had more to say about the Steps since writing *Becoming a New Person.* I already believed that the relevance of the Steps went beyond the addiction and recovery movement. But I didn't want to do as many other authors have done — write the same book in two or three different ways under different titles. I do not believe that is the case with *Twelve Steps to Spiritual Wholeness: A Christian Pathway.*

So, what's different about this book?

Well, first of all, I'm eight years older and, hopefully, wiser than when I wrote *Becoming a New Person.* During those eight years, I have participated in hundreds of therapy groups and presented scores of workshops and retreats on the Twelve Steps throughout the country. I believe these experiences have contributed to a deeper understanding of the human condition and the role the Steps play in helping us lead a better life.

Second, *Twelve Steps to Spiritual Wholeness* develops the psychological dimension of the spiritual journey more fully than the previous book. It points out the dynamics of shame, resentment, and fear more specifically. It also describes more fully the workings of the false-self system, which would have us become okay by *doing* the "right things." *Becoming a New Person,* on the other hand, takes a more theological approach, speaking of sin, grace, salvation, the seven deadly sins, cardinal virtues, supernatural virtues, and other themes found in the mystical wisdom of the Church. The theological approach, while not totally absent, is given less prominence in *Twelve Steps to Spiritual Wholeness.* In that sense, then, most people will probably find their experiences better named in this book.

For those reasons, *Twelve Steps to Spiritual Wholeness* and *Becoming a New Person* can be viewed as companion works for helping Christians use the Twelve Steps as a pathway to the abundant life that Jesus promised us. (See John 10:10.)

How to Work With the Twelve Steps

We can approach the Twelve Steps from a philosophical/ theological standpoint, searching for what they imply about human nature and locating parallel themes in Christianity. These implications and themes are then compared with a psychological or therapeutic approach to transformation. This approach has merit. More discussion of it needs to take place in the Church if we are to use the Twelve Steps in a Christian context. As things stand, far too much distinction is made between spirituality and religion. Christianity, being a religion, and the Twelve Steps, presenting itself as a spirituality, are often compared and contrasted with each other. Although many Christians have embraced the Steps as a way to live the Christian spiritual life, they generally find themselves speaking a different language about spirituality than Christians who are not explicitly working the Steps. My own view is that the Church needs to use the Twelve Steps as a way to help people grow spiritually. On the other hand, people working the Steps need to hear what the Church has to say about human nature and the spiritual journey. Without sound teaching, the spiritual journey cannot go very far. Without a spirituality of conversion, however, there will be no one interested in the teaching.

The second way to approach the Twelve Steps, the one adopted in this book, is to use them as a way to grow. We might call this an existential response to the Steps. This response involves *working* the Steps and so coming to the wisdom that can only be found through *experience.* The existential approach sees the Steps as a guide to the spiritual life, spelling out in systematic fashion the work that must be done to break free from negative and sinful influences in our lives. By doing this work, we come, as Step Twelve promises, to a spiritual awakening, an awareness of our true self in God, and we know what it means to be fully human.

The best way to work the Steps is in the context of a small peer-support group of people who are motivated to grow. Appendix One provides a format for Christian Twelve Step groups. If such a group is not available, then get with a friend and start one! Failing that, I suggest that you attend one of the many kinds of Twelve Step group meetings found throughout the country. Alcoholics Anonymous, Al-Anon, Overeaters Anonymous, Adult Children of Alcoholics, and Codependents Anonymous meetings can be found in almost all medium-sized towns. If you've never been to such a meeting, call and find out when an open meeting is scheduled. Go to at least ten meetings before forming a judgment about what's going on.

It is also helpful to work the Steps under the guidance of someone experienced in spiritual matters. This is the value of the *sponsor* in Twelve Step groups and of the *spiritual director* in Christian spirituality. Such a person is not a guru or someone who will tell you what to do. He or she is a sounding board or soul companion on the spiritual journey. This is a person with whom you can share your formal Step work, someone who can suggest good reading materials, maybe even someone to give you feedback about how they perceive your behavior. It is difficult to go very far without such a friend, but, sadly, many attempt to travel the spiritual way without one. Much of the resistance to seeking this guidance comes from the proud ego, which wants to work the Steps "my way."

If you cannot find a group or a companion for the journey right away, it will still be of value to begin working the Steps on your own. Just do keep asking, searching, and knocking on the doors of the Spirit for the gift of self-honesty. Honesty is something the ego knows nothing about, and it is very difficult to learn by oneself. So keep looking for a group of some kind and for a spiritual companion to help you grow in honesty.

Initially, I suggest that people go through the Steps one at a time, doing some kind of formal reflection to learn the lessons of that Step. After going through all the Steps, it will be obvious that some of them are worked on occasion, while others are reference points for daily living. Eventually, it will become clear that the Twelve Steps are essential for staying properly focused in the spiritual journey. It takes time, however (at least two years), to learn to use the Steps as a rhythm for daily living. Give yourself this time. The blessing will be yours!

CHAPTER ONE

Admitting Our Powerlessness

STEP ONE

**We admitted we were powerless over [sin] —
that our lives had become unmanageable.**

It seems everywhere we go these days, we hear people talking about the Twelve Steps or "The Program." Some social commentators have called Twelve Step groups the most significant spiritual movement in the twentieth century.

The primary reason for the popularity of the Twelve Steps is that more people than ever are being exposed to them through addiction-treatment programs. In a medium-sized city like Baton Rouge, Louisiana, where I formerly practiced, more than a thousand families participate in professional treatment programs each year. Virtually all addiction therapists recommend follow-up participation in a Twelve Step group for their clients. If you multiply the Baton Rouge experience by the number of other cities providing treatment services, you get hundreds of thousands of people becoming familiar with the Twelve Steps each year.

Make no mistake, there is nothing magical about the Steps. They simply list in a systematic way the work we must do to allow God to work more fully in our lives. But it is precisely this breaking things down into small achievable goals that constitutes the great value of the Steps. These Steps give us a "handle" on the spiritual life.

The key to the entire Twelve Step program lies in Step One: *We admitted we were powerless over [sin] — that our lives had become unmanageable.*

Most people working the Twelve Steps have identified some compulsion that causes problems for themselves and others. Usually, they tried on their own to control the compulsive behavior but never attained more than short-term success. They used their will power against it, tried "mind over matter," and prayed for help. Nothing worked!

Feeling hopeless about this enslavement, they enter a treatment program or join a Twelve Step group. There they learn that chronic addictions cannot, in fact, be controlled by one's own will. So the logical question is, if reason and will power can't correct things, what can?

The answer to this question is that where reason and will power fail, surrender and "seeing" will succeed. The spirit of Step One says, "You can't control your compulsion, so why not stop trying? See how many ways you have tried and failed. Quit pretending things aren't all that bad, that somehow you can make them better. In other words, be completely honest about what has happened in your life as a result of this compulsive behavior. Only then will you create a space within where the power of the Spirit can work."

Powerlessness and Sin

Step One presents a paradox, saying that the way to regain control of our life is to give up trying to control it — to throw in the towel and admit defeat. This doesn't make sense at first, but later it will be seen as the beginning of wisdom.

Step One has relevance beyond the addiction and recovery movement, for the power of sin creates havoc in all our lives.

These days, *sin* is an unpopular word connoting unhealthy guilt and shame. But the authors of the New Testament recognized sin as a power able to move us toward nonloving selfish behavior. This power worked through culture (the world), our internalized conditioning (the flesh), and preternatural spirits (the Devil). For most of us, the concrete experience of sin is our own selfishness and reluctance to relate. Who among us can deny this experience?

Another insight to be found in Scripture says that we cannot reverse our selfish tendencies by our own will. In his Letter to the Romans, Saint Paul speaks of how he wants to do good but cannot find the power to do so. A point he makes again and again is that liberation from sin does not come from keeping the law. In fact, law keepers frequently become self-righteous about their goodness and judgmental of others. Such was the case with the religious authorities who condemned Jesus to death in the name of the law.

A sinner, then, might be described as one whose life is ruled by selfishness. Using the addiction model, we would say that a sinner is one who is compulsively selfish — in other words, resistant to loving relationships. This selfish direction of the will demonstrates itself in specific acts of behavior, which we call personal sins. Most personal sins are not planned or calculated but happen compulsively when we feel threatened in some manner. However, these sins bring consequences to us and to others.

The Roots of Selfishness

Until we become consciously committed to living by the Spirit, selfishness will rule our hearts. For addicts in recovery, this truth is obvious. It is the drinking or gambling or desire to control others that ruled the heart. For those whose lives have not been torn asunder by addiction, it may be more difficult to get in touch with the roots of selfishness.

In beginning to examine your heart for evidence of selfishness, ask yourself, "What makes me tick? What do I really want out of life? What upsets me when I am denied it?"

Most of us, when reflecting on these questions, will find that our selfishness is directed toward one or more of five passions: pleasure, power, status, security, and esteem. There are legitimate ways to meet these needs, but selfishness makes them the very centers of meaning and value.

People can live years selfishly pursuing pleasure, power, status, security, and esteem. In the end, however, none of these bring happiness, for they are conditional achievements — they can be taken away at any time. Empty though they are, the world holds them out as roads to human fulfillment, and many there are who travel these roads.

Happily, God has created us in such a manner that we cannot find true happiness apart from living in the Spirit. As Saint Augustine put it, "Thou has created us for thyself, O Lord, and our hearts will not rest until they rest in thee." It would be wonderful if we could live this truth from the beginning of our lives until the end. Most of us, however, travel the selfish road for a while, flirting superficially with the spiritual life but never surrendering our selfish center until we grow tired of it.

The selfish road leads to broken relationships and inner emptiness. Whatever material gains we make are bracketed by anxiety, for the economy could fail and leave us with nothing.

Other consequences of selfishness are described by Saint Paul in Galatians: "…immorality, impurity, licentiousness, idolatry, sorcery, hatreds, rivalry, jealousy, outbursts of fury, acts of selfishness, dissensions, factions, occasions of envy, drinking bouts, orgies, and the like. I warn you, as I warned you before, that those who do such things will not inherit the kingdom of God" (5:19-21). In fact, this description sounds like the lifestyle of one in hell.

Paradoxically, it is the unhappiness of our selfish ways that can lead us to commit our lives to God in earnest. Some, it seems, must go through considerable pain before coming around; others learn by observing the consequences of selfishness experienced by others. But none among us is immune to the insidious powers of sin, and none among us has escaped from selfish tendencies.

It is no coincidence that the first beatitude taught by Jesus is "Blessed are the poor in spirit, for theirs is the kingdom of heaven" (Matthew 5:3). Who are these poor in spirit?

They are the people who know their need for God — who have learned that "their way" does not bring true happiness. This is what addiction teaches some people and what selfishness teaches all of us.

There are two types of people who realize poverty of spirit. The first are those who have been beaten up by life through social injustice, addiction, divorce, or other problems. Through these experiences, they learn their inability to control things.

The second type is the person committed to living a life of love. In the struggle to love, we discover the immensity of our selfishness and our need for the Spirit to help us overcome this selfishness.

The critical importance of poverty of spirit is that until we embrace it, the Spirit will do little to help us. If we are not poor in spirit, then we are rich in our own sense of power and self-importance. We are like the "healthy" people in the gospels whom Christ could not cure because they did not believe they were sick. (See Mark 2:17.)

We are all sick! We were created to know love, peace of mind, creative enterprise, and harmony with the earth and other creatures. But deep down inside, most of us are filled with fear, and we use selfish "fixes" to stay out of touch with this fear. The fear, however, cannot go away until we allow the Spirit entrance into our hearts.

Practicing Step One

The best way to cultivate poverty of spirit is to practice honesty. This is difficult, for it means we must get in touch with the dark side of our nature as well as our true strengths. We examine our center to see what we are living for. We note the consequences to ourselves and others that come from this center. We pay attention to our thinking process and trace our thoughts to our deepest desires. We acknowledge our selfishness, and we see how fear motivates us to this selfishness.

Reflecting in this way, we begin to bring the darkness in our hearts into the light where it can be healed. This process can be painful, but it is a sweet pain, and there is new life within it.

It is good to work the Steps with others. Sharing your first step with a group, a spiritual director, or a trusted friend is the best way to benefit from this work. If you do not have a small group to meet with, Appendix One gives instructions to help you get one started.

Questions for Reflection

1. What makes you tick? What criteria do you usually employ when making decisions? What does this teach you about your center of meaning and value?

2. How do you experience powerlessness in your life? What kinds of problems/situations have you tried to change again and again, but to no avail? What are the consequences to you? To others?

3. How do you experience selfishness in your life? How have you tried to reverse your selfish behavior? Have these strategies been successful?
4. If you could change anything about yourself, what would you most like to change? Why?

CHAPTER TWO

Trusting in a Higher Power

STEP TWO

Came to believe that a Power greater than ourselves could restore us to sanity.

What is the meaning of life? Why are we here on this earth? Is there something in particular we should be doing? What is death? Is there anything after death? What is good? What is evil? How can life have meaning if death and evil exist?

These are questions all human beings must struggle with at one time or another. There is no indication that other animals are troubled about these issues; they are just themselves, living out of instinct and conditioning, one day at a time. We must be careful that we do not become creatures of mere instinct and conditioning. By allowing ourselves to struggle with questions pertaining to the higher meaning of life, we begin to experience our deepest levels of humanity. That is what Step Two of the Twelve Step program of recovery invites us to do.

People using the Twelve Steps as a process for recovery from addictions begin to work with Step Two after working Step One. In Step One they came to recognize how addictively pursuing pleasure, security, power, status, and esteem brings short-term relief and long-term pain. Step One teaches us that we do not control life and that willful behavior leads to misery. This sobering insight that can lead to poverty of spirit can also open us to grace.

We cannot stop here, however. Recognizing that the old false centers of meaning brought misery is helpful. However, if false centers are all we have ever known, then renouncing them feels like renouncing our very soul. This can be traumatic.

That's where Step Two comes in. This Step affirms that there is a way to live that brings sanity. This sanity is not the fruit of a controlling willfulness but of adapting oneself to life's higher meaning.

To the addict who has given up what feels like everything, Step Two is extremely challenging. Many people have distorted religious beliefs; some have even had negative experiences of religion. That is why, in Twelve Step programs, recovering addicts are simply asked to affirm some kind of Power greater than themselves rather than a particular religious creed. For many, this Power is simply found within the support group, but most affirm the existence of God. Such an affirmation in a greater Power is a starting point for developing a new, unselfish vision of life.

Faith and Reason

The spiritual movement emphasized in Step Two is well known to Christianity. In his classical treatise *The Grammar of*

Assent, John Henry Cardinal Newman makes a distinction between the assent of the intellect and the assent of the will. The former movement corresponds to Step Two, the latter to Step Three, which we shall discuss in the next chapter. The two movements are related and form an essential part of faith, but there is a difference between intellectual and volitional conviction.

The importance of intellectual conviction cannot be overstated. There are many times on the spiritual journey when we do not feel God's presence. During these times of darkness and transition, it is reason that prompts us to remain faithful. Those who lack an intellectual conviction can be likened to the characters in Jesus' parable of the Sower who were shallow and superficial or weak in conviction and who allowed the cares of the world to undermine their faith. (See Matthew 13:1-23.) Without intellectual conviction, we flounder or give up on the journey entirely.

Mature Christian faith is not blind. Faith will never last if it goes against reason. Trust based on anti-intellectual positions is no Christian virtue. There are many reasons to believe that Jesus is God's holy one, and there are many reasons for doubt. In the last analysis, faith can be supported by reason, but it is not the outcome of rational reflection. Faith transcends reason, opening the mind to a more intuitive kind of awareness of God's reality in our lives. Faith knows, but it does not know how it knows. However, its knowing cannot violate the rational function or the mind will become overly disturbed.

Jesus as Our Hope

A bumper sticker commonly observed a few years ago read, "Jesus is the answer." When I worked in campus ministry, we put this slogan on a chalkboard during retreats. Returning from a break one day, we noticed that someone had written beneath the slogan, "If Jesus is the answer, then what is the question?"

Although we had another scheduled activity to begin, I thought it worthwhile for the group to spend a little time with this question.

"What are the questions Jesus answers for you? How does he answer them? Are there still questions and issues for which you have no answers?" These are the questions I asked the students to discuss. I had them complete the assignment by compiling a list of questions that Jesus answers. Here is what they came up with: *Does God exist? What is God like? Is there life after death? Does evil have the last word? Is there a proper way for human beings to live?* Perhaps you could add your own questions to this list.

Jesus answers these questions with his own life, teaching, death, and Resurrection. He is not an academic theoretician offering tentative speculations about these issues. Rather, he spoke about them with authority; he knew what he was talking about. In the end, his authority was put to the test by the powers of evil, and he emerged victorious on Easter morning.

Because of Jesus' Resurrection, we can affirm with Saint Paul that "neither death, nor life, nor angels, nor principalities, nor present things, nor future things, nor powers, nor height, nor depth, nor any other creature will be able to separate us from the love of God in Christ Jesus our Lord" (Romans 8:38-39).

This is very good news indeed! Do we believe it?

The word *nothing* deserves our careful consideration here. Do we believe that nothing can separate us from God's love? Step Two invites us to hold to the absolute conviction that God's love is available to us at all times and is capable of overcoming any obstacles that prevent our realizing this.

Peace Beyond Understanding

Once we make Christ the center of our lives, things begin to fall into place. Those nagging existential questions that had been polluting our mind with fear, doubt, and confusion begin to go away. Our minds become more peaceful. We discover that we have more energy to live without this fear, doubt, and confusion keeping us preoccupied. This is, I believe, the basis for that part of Step Two that speaks of living in sanity.

Peace of mind is a gift that Christ promises to all Christians. "Peace I leave with you; my peace I give to you. Not as the world gives do I give it to you. Do not let your hearts be troubled or afraid" (John 14:27). He does not promise us wealth or health or fame. The peace he gives transcends these and other worldly contingencies for peace of mind.

How many people today need this peace of mind! How many — Christians included — are troubled in spirit! Could it be that many in the Church are caught up in worldly standards for attaining peace and happiness?

There are troubles in life, to be sure. No one goes through life without experiencing grief, disappointment, guilt, and hurt. Can we have troubles without being troubled or disturbed? That, it seems to me, is one of the important issues that Step Two addresses.

Saint Paul had many troubles. In his Second Letter to the Corinthians, he recounts some of the incredible hardships he had to endure because he was an apostle. Even so, he was able to say, "I am content with weaknesses, insults, hardships, persecutions, and constraints, for the sake of Christ; for when I am weak, then I am strong" (12:10). So it is with the person who believes that nothing can separate him or her from the love of God.

Working Step Two

The Twelve Steps are not goals to be attained and then forgotten. They are guideposts on the spiritual journey. As such, they must be worked time and again. This is expressly true for Step Two. Every day we must return to this step to affirm the meaning of our lives and the basis of our hope in Christ Jesus, especially during times of doubt and confusion.

The best way to begin working Step Two is to examine your own religious questions honestly, then see how your belief in Jesus addresses these issues. Many Catholics need to update their faith understanding. They have adult questions about life, but they haven't updated the beliefs they were taught as children. It is troublesome, to be sure, to examine and update our beliefs, but the results of such an effort are extremely worthwhile.

We can work on Step Two by reading Scripture. Faith comes from hearing the Word of God, wrote Saint Paul. (See Romans 10:17.) By reading the Scriptures, we implant in our minds the beliefs that strengthen our conviction to follow Christ.

Another excellent way to work on Step Two is to study the teachings of the Church. This can be done through reading or by attending a discussion series on this topic. The teachings of the Church represent centuries of reflection on the meaning of Scripture and, as such, they root our beliefs in solid ground.

It is also important to give up negative influences on our thinking. We do not benefit from books, magazines, and television viewing that promote a value system at odds with the gospel; these influences undermine our convictions in insidious ways.

Neither do we benefit from spending much time with people who have negative, cynical attitudes. Granted, if this is a family member, it may be impossible to avoid this kind of contact. However, we can make an effort to avoid negative people with whom we are not forced by familial or other circumstances to associate.

On the other hand, it is important to spend time with people who are excited about the gospel, for something of their positive attitudes will infect us. Indeed, the best way to work Step Two, and all the other steps, is in the context of a Christian community, for it is in community that faith flourishes.

Questions for Reflection

1. How has your belief about God changed since you were a child?
2. How does Christ fit into your understanding of God?
3. What part of the Christian faith is hardest for you to believe?
4. How does belief in God give you a sense of hope about your life?

CHAPTER THREE

Centering in God

STEP THREE

Made a decision to turn our will and our lives over to the care of God *as we understood Him.*

The first three of the Twelve Steps summarize the spiritual dynamics of conversion. In Step One, we come to recognize our limitations. In Step Two, we affirm our hope in God. In Step Three, we surrender our lives to God. Step One says, "I can't…"; Step Two says, "God can…"; and Step Three says, "I will let God do it."

The shift is from centeredness in self to centeredness in God. We learn to let go of self-will and let God guide our lives. This essentially is what is meant when Scripture speaks of *metanoia,* or change of heart.

Who Is Your God?

In his Sermon on the Mount, Jesus tells us, "Do not store up for yourselves treasures on earth, where moth and decay destroy, and thieves break in and steal. But store up treasures in heaven, where neither moth nor decay destroys, nor thieves break in and steal. For where your treasure is, there also will your heart be" (Matthew 6:19-21).

Each of us has what Jesus and Scripture call a heart. The heart as understood here is not the physical organ but the deepest source of our thoughts, feelings, and desires. The heart is our center of meaning and value. What we think about most and desire most deeply, that is our treasure. And where our treasure is, there is our "god." Jesus tells us that if our treasure is anything less than God, it can be taken away from us.

Nothing demonstrates the truth of Jesus' statement more than addiction. As their disease progresses, addicts become more and more centered on their "fix." The alcoholic thinks about and desires alcohol more than anything else. Codependents think about and desire to control other people more than they think about their own health. This is true for other addictive involvements as well. This fix is a kind of treasure, for it brings temporary relief from pain. In the long run, however, it destroys everything — serenity, money, mental and physical health, family, and more. Addictive fixes are earthly treasures that corrode the heart — and the person.

There are earthly treasures more subtle than addictive fixes, some of which we discussed in our reflections on Step One. We can become centered on pleasure, power, security, status, success, and even esteem. In the long run, each of these centers brings big problems. Human nature being what it is, God is the only center that will bring us peace of mind and long-term happiness.

Do we believe this? Do we believe that God is our only happiness? This is the critical question of faith. We discover our answer by examining what our treasure is, what we are looking to for our happiness.

Surrender of the Will

Step Three invites us to surrender our wills to the care of God. How do we do this?

In the previous chapter, we referred to the classical essay by John Henry Cardinal Newman, *The Grammar of Assent*. Newman made a distinction between surrender of the intellect and surrender of the will. It is difficult to sustain a surrender of the will if the intellect does not cooperate.

That is why Step Two, with its emphasis on belief and hope, is so important. We need to read, to meditate upon, and to affirm our hope to keep our minds convinced of the importance of centering in God. However, this alone will not be enough to sustain us.

It might help to clarify what we mean by the will. By will, we mean the orientation of our freedom. As human beings, we are free to do this or to do that. We do not *surrender* our freedom, for God would not accept it. A chief distinction between authentic religion and cultism is that cults require the surrender of freedom. God does not want this. God leaves us free because freedom is the only appropriate context for love.

What we do surrender is the direction we would like our freedom to take. We enter into a covenant in which we ask God to direct our freedom toward a relationship with him and to reveal to us his will. We undertake this pursuit of God's will in freedom.

Before the surrender of our will takes place, the "I" of self-will runs our lives. After surrender, we have a sense of "we" inside — God and I. We place our will at God's disposal, and he leads us to become the people he created us to be. He does this through Christ, who shows us the will of God for human beings.

As Christians, we surrender our lives to Christ, the bridge between the transcendent God and humanity. In our surrender, we become cells in the Mystical Body of Christ. We begin to live by the life of his Body and not our own. Living by the life of his Body, we become the people he created us to be.

Surrender of Our Lives

It is important to mention both surrender of our wills and surrender of our lives. Some Christian denominations maintain that a surrender of the will alone guarantees our heavenly reward. By emphasizing the importance of surrendering our *lives,* however, we acknowledge that our surrender must be ongoing.

Surrender of the will moves us from "I" to "we." Because there is still an "I" in this "we," we must commit ourselves daily to the care of Christ. As anyone on the spiritual journey knows, it is entirely possible to move from "we" back to "I" through neglect of prayer and spiritual discipline. Christ comes when we invite him, but he will not stay if we do not want him. During the early part of the spiritual journey, this movement from "I" to "we" and back to "I" happens many times. Each time it happens, we feel more and more lonely and unhappy. We miss our soul partner and learn all over again the hard lesson of Step One — the futility of willful living. As we persist in the journey through ongoing surrender, "we" becomes a more consistent experience.

Surrender of our lives also points out the importance of bringing our lifestyle into conformity with God's will. Recovering alcoholics are told by AA that they must change playgrounds and playmates if they are to stay sober. This advice is true for all of us. We must not think that the spiritual life is simply a personal and private matter with no connection to our lifestyle. It will be difficult to maintain an attitude of willingness toward God if we do not change certain aspects of our lives.

What kind of job do we have? Why do we do this work? How

do we spend our money? How much time do we spend with our family? How do we treat the poor? What are we doing to share our gifts in our church community?

These are important questions, for they challenge us to examine how our surrender is taking root in the everyday affairs of life. If we hold back in any area, there is still a lack of surrender.

The Inner Struggle

Surrendering our wills and our lives to God is an ongoing process and one we shall fail at many times. But we do not lose heart. Christ knows who we are and remains close to us through our struggles. If we push him out of our soul through an outburst of willfulness, he will not go away forever. He waits patiently for our next invitation. For Catholics, the sacrament of reconciliation (penance) is an opportunity to celebrate these falls and reunions.

The movement from "I" to "we" creates a kind of inner civil war. People who are not aware of this civil war are either so totally into "I" that they cannot experience any will but their own or else they are so far along in the journey that the willfulness of "I" has been burned away. Most of us, however, are acutely aware of the clash between our wills and God's.

While frustrating at times, this awareness of inner struggle is a positive sign. We would not even be aware of it were Christ not challenging us within. Knowing this is helpful, for it indicates that transformation is taking place.

Through this struggle, Christ will put to death the false self and bring to birth a new person created in his image. This is a process modern psychology knows little about, for it is a movement of grace. We could never accomplish with ourselves what Christ will accomplish if we persist in our surrender and allow him to work with us. The result will be a person more beautiful than we could ever create through self-education, goals, and resolution. In heaven there are no "self-made" beings, only Christs. The inner struggles felt through Steps One, Two, and Three are birth pangs of becoming new Christs.

Loving in the Spirit

In everyday life, living Step Three means we must commit ourselves to a life of love. God is love, and we who are created in God's image and likeness are most ourselves when we love. The inner struggle discussed above is a conflict between our will to love and our will to selfishness. Our best response is to let go of what we cannot control — our residual self-will — and let Christ work with it. He knows us, and he works toward our transformation as quickly as possible. To change too quickly, however, would not be good for us. Christ knows the best schedule for us, so we let him do his own work in his own time.

On a positive note, we are already acting like new persons in Christ whenever we love. He teaches us to love by giving us his Spirit. As he lives in us through faith and the Eucharist, Christ continues to love the Father. This love of Christ for the Father is the Holy Spirit.

For Christians, there are two stages in the surrender of the will. First is the surrender of our heart (or center) to Christ through faith. We know almost nothing about the unmanifest Father, but we can relate to the manifest begotten Son. Going from self-centeredness to Christ-centeredness is a first movement of surrender.

The second stage is allowing ourselves to experience not only Christ's love for us, which is wonderful, but also his love for the Father — unquestionably the greatest love in the universe. This opportunity to experience the love of the Trinity "from the inside" is the unique dimension of Christian faith.

Practically speaking, the surrender to Christ and the opening to the Spirit may take place at different stages in our growth. In the early Church, these two were celebrated in baptism and then through the laying on of hands by an apostle. In our own lives, we experience the Holy Spirit by asking Christ to open us to receive this gift. If, for example, we have difficulty loving one another, we can ask Christ to help us with his Spirit, whose love is far greater than our own. This learning to love with Christ's own love is the goal of the spiritual journey. It is the beginning of heaven — or life in the Trinity — a life that will never die.

Questions for Reflection

1. How do you experience God's presence in your life?
2. What does it mean to you to surrender your will to the care of God? How do you do this?
3. What does it mean to you to surrender your life to the care of God? How do you do this?
4. How does the Holy Spirit fit into your understanding of God?

CHAPTER FOUR

Knowing Ourselves

STEP FOUR

**Made a searching and fearless
moral inventory of ourselves.**

The great spiritual writers often stress the importance of self-knowledge. This foundational virtue is synonymous in many writings with the virtue of humility. True humility is not self-renunciation but self-honesty, which leads to self-knowledge.

Authentic humility helps us recognize not only our weaknesses but also our strengths. There can be no true self-knowledge where we overemphasize either side. A problem arises, for example, if we possess so little self-esteem that we are afraid to acknowledge weaknesses and failures. Such fear leads us to overemphasize our strong points and shy away from encounters that bring criticism or disapproval. These strategies don't work in the long run, nor do they bring us true spiritual liberation.

The real wisdom of the Twelve Step process is in the placement of Step Four. As we worked Steps One and Two, we began to experience a shift from a false center of meaning to centeredness in God. In Step Three, we turned our wills and our lives over to God's care and discovered God's unconditional love.

The realization of this love gives us the courage to look honestly at ourselves, for no matter what we discover, it will not change God's love for us. Our self-respect does not depend upon our being perfect or deserving of approval.

Values and Choices

What are our moral values? How does our behavior express these values? Where do we fall short? Step Four is concerned with all these issues.

The first is the hardest. Many of us live according to values we never truly examined. We perceive these values as "shoulds, musts, and oughts." They sit on our shoulders as judges, observing all we do, ever ready to convict us for the slightest deviation from the straight and narrow. Even when we do all we "should," there is no true serenity — only an uneasy truce with guilt.

As adults, it is inappropriate for us to base our lives on trying to do what we "should do." Rather, we do certain things because we believe in their value and are committed to directing our lives accordingly. For example, we either go to Mass on Sunday because it is a law of the Church and our parents taught us that we should, or we go because we recognize the value of giving praise and thanks to God in community as well as the value of unity with Christ in the Eucharist. We are more likely to behave according to values we believe in than values that are thrust upon us. The journey from "I should" to "I choose to" means leaving childish ways behind and becoming adult Christians. It's not an easy journey. It takes time and considerable struggle to decide for ourselves what we truly believe.

Step Four helps facilitate this process. In doing our inventory, we are likely to recognize values that are still on the level of "shoulds" and, having recognized this, ask ourselves whether we really believe in this value.

Choosing to do something feels different than doing something because we should. Behaving according to self-chosen values leaves us feeling true to ourselves rather than to others. Going against our own self-chosen values is more difficult than going against someone else's values. (Rebelliousness is usually directed against others.) While it is possible for us to go against our chosen values, the guilt we experience is quite different. We feel remorse when we violate our own values; we feel ashamed when we break the rules of others. Remorse is more likely to lead us to reconciliation.

Some will no doubt object to the idea of "self-chosen values," especially where those values concern God's commandments. Of course, we obey the commandments because God says we should. But when we keep them because we recognize their value in teaching us to live a good life, we know we are well along on the spiritual journey. With the psalmist we may exclaim:

Though distress and anguish have come upon me,
    your commands are my delight.
Your decrees are forever just;
    give me discernment that I may live.

(Psalm 119:143-144)

The Inventory

Many older Catholics will remember doing their examination of conscience in preparation for confession. The process of Step Four is similar except that it invites us to be searching and fearless in our self-examination. Let us say, then, that Step Four is a very special preparation for an in-depth confession — a general "housecleaning," as it were.

In working Step Four, it is preferable to write things down. The various Twelve Step programs have developed work sheets and workbooks to facilitate the inventory. Whichever format you have, the act of writing is important. For those who have no workbook, I have included a suggested format at the end of this chapter. Through the years, I have listened to hundreds of people share their Fourth Step inventories as part of their Fifth Step. Those who made a written preparation were much more in touch with their lives than those who had not. There is something about the process of writing that slows down our thinking and enables us to remember things we had pushed into the subconscious. Many times people have shared with me that they thought they didn't have much to write about until they started writing. Then it all came back to them.

Because the writing process could be long and involved, it is best to do your inventory in several sittings rather than all at once. When your mind and your writing hand get tired, take a break. Carry a small notebook with you and jot down insights and memories that continue to come to you. There is also nothing wrong with revising what you've written as you go along. Take as much time as you need. Most people spend a week or two working on Step Four. Some take even longer. The words *searching* and *fearless* are most significant here. Who is this person living this life? It takes time and courage to get in touch with yourself.

Those who take an inventory such as the one that follows will surely grow in awareness. This awareness in itself is a great value. To be awake or asleep — this is the choice confronting all of us. Most people are somewhere in-between — not totally asleep but not really awake.

People avoid waking up, I am convinced, because they are afraid to experience the pains they carry within. Little pain is felt during sleep, while living with our eyes open is often painful. Twelve Step spirituality does not promise freedom from pain; making a good Fourth Step most likely *will* be painful. But the Steps provide the process for resolving that pain and healing our brokenness. We do not stop with the awareness and self-knowledge gained in Step Four but move on in the Steps to ground this awareness in loving relationships.

A Suggested Format

For each of the values listed below, answer the following questions:

- What does this value mean to me? How is it put into practice?
- How has my behavior expressed this value in a positive manner? Give at least two or three examples.
- How has my behavior gone against what I believe this value calls for? Give as many examples as come to mind — especially incidents about which you feel guilt, shame, resentment, or fear.

Values From the Ten Commandments

1. Putting God first.
2. Reverence for the name of God.
3. Keeping holy the Lord's day.
4. Respect for parents.
5. Restraint from violence toward others.
6. Chastity in sexual relationships.
7. Honesty in dealing with others.
8. Honesty in speech.
9. Fidelity in relationships.
10. Being content with material possessions.

Values From the Cardinal Virtues

11. Moderation in the use of food, drink, material goods.
12. Taking responsibility for meeting your own needs.
13. Working for justice.
14. Standing up for your beliefs.

Values From Works of Mercy

15. Helping those in need of food, drink, clothing, shelter.
16. Visiting the sick.
17. Visiting prisoners.
18. Forgiving others the wrongs done you.
19. Exercising patience.
20. Comforting others when they are troubled.

These twenty values are much esteemed in Christianity. They provide a profile of love that, when followed, will enable us to experience the love of God in our lives.

Questions for Reflection

1. What kinds of "shoulds" in your life keep you feeling guilty and pressured?
2. Give an example of how you have transferred a value in your life from "I should" to "I choose."
3. How do you feel about doing the inventory suggested in this chapter? What do you think you gain by this?
4. What is more difficult to identify: your strengths or your failings? Explain.

CHAPTER FIVE

Admitting Our Wrongs

STEP FIVE

Admitted to God, to ourselves and to another human being the exact nature of our wrongs.

Unconditional love is the only true source of human happiness. When we do not experience unconditional love, we tend to view all love as conditional, love with strings attached. We believe we are loved only because we are smart or good-looking or responsible or helpful or wealthy — or whatever. This leads us to pursue intelligence, good looks, helpfulness, wealth, or other artifices as ways to earn love. We believe we cannot be lovable unless we do the right things or possess the right qualities. We doubt our innate lovableness and we are unhappy.

Research in child development has shown that the perception of conditional love may come at a very early age — even in the womb. No parent intends this, of course, but often parents are human beings who, having experienced conditional love themselves, bring to parenthood the dynamics of love as something that has to be earned. To avoid being hurt, the child reacts to this conditional love by drawing back in a defensive posture, and this is the beginning of unhappiness.

Although children usually enjoy a special union with God, it is a relationship directly identified with the parental relationship. As children withdraw from their parents in a defensive posture, their image of God becomes distorted.

As we mature and continue to experience conditional love, we build defenses to avoid getting hurt. To "earn" the love of others, we try to be good, perfect, unemotional, in control, smart, and so forth. The more we get caught up in this, the more we lose touch with our true center, which is God. Eventually, we become focused on the false centers mentioned in Step One: security, pleasure, power, status, esteem, control, and other worldly attractions. We attach ourselves to these false centers in the hope that they will make us happy and peaceful, that they will make us okay.

Whatever payoffs we gain through these attempts are short-lived; in the end, these false centers make us unhappy.

The process described above demonstrates how the power of sin becomes rooted in each of us. Sin separates us from God, from other people, and from our own deepest, truest nature. Sin is *diabolos,* the splitting power. It begins with the perception that there are conditions to being loved, and from there it leads us to center our lives on worldly values.

Understanding the roots of our malady can help us recognize what we need to be healed. If conditional love is ultimately the problem, then it follows that unconditional love is ultimately the cure we need. But how do we come to recognize the fact that we are loved unconditionally?

It helps to know at least one person who accepts us as we are — even in our messiness, selfishness, imperfection, and brokenness. If just one person can love us with no strings attached, we will conclude more easily that we are lovable. Step Five is our opportunity to find unconditional love and acceptance from another person.

Letting Go

The first five steps in the program are about opening our lives to the acceptance of unconditional love. In Step One, we let go of false centers that keep us attached to a lifestyle of conditional love. In Step Two, we affirm our hope in God's loving care for us. In Step Three, we surrender our spiritual center to God's care. The moral inventory of Step Four allows us to be honest with ourselves about our values and how we have been living.

Then comes Step Five. Here we are asked to tell God, ourselves, and another human person the exact nature of our wrongs. We do this by sharing our Step Four inventory with God and with another person. For most of us, this is a frightening prospect. Step Five asks us to bare our souls to another human being. If we have done this in the past only to be put down, we question whether that might happen again.

It is not supposed to. The one who hears our Fifth Step is supposed to listen, accept, and validate in a nonjudgmental way the experiences we share. He or she may also offer moral or spiritual counseling, but this too should be done in a nonjudgmental manner.

Through the years, I have listened to hundreds of Fifth Steps. Those sharing were usually nervous at first, but eventually it would begin to seem that they weren't talking to me at all; they were just talking, aware that someone was listening. The relief of confession and unburdening had come to them. They wanted to leave nothing out.

What amazes me most is how much abuse there is in so many of our homes. Grown men cry because they were beaten as children, and now they beat their own children and don't know how to stop. Women cry for their aborted children; young adults lament the loss of their chastity. Almost everyone who shared their Fifth Step gave testimony to an enormous capacity for self-deception. After they had told all, they were younger, freer, happier — as if they had rejoined the human race.

The Fifth Step Counselor

The Fifth Step is a chance for us to get honest about ourselves and our life, and this in itself is a healing experience. Quite obviously, however, we cannot be this open and vulnerable with just anyone. Most people choose to do the Fifth Step with their minister or their Twelve Step sponsor. The Fifth Steps I have heard were at a treatment center where I worked as a counselor with training in spirituality.

It is not a good idea to do the Fifth Step with a spouse. We need to be free to talk about the hurts and frustrations even in our marriage. After doing Step Five with a qualified counselor, we can share some of it with our spouse — but always with discretion. There are things that could hurt a relationship unnecessarily. Most Fifth Step counselors agree that hearing Fifth Steps is a humbling experience. As I listened, it never occurred to me to act as a judge. What these people shared, I, too, had experienced or done or come close to doing at one time or another.

Sacramental Reconciliation

A Fifth Step is not exactly the same as the Catholic sacrament of penance and reconciliation, although it may be shared in this context. Where the sacrament focuses on sin and reassurance of God's forgiveness, the Fifth Step covers much more ground. Sinful situations are discussed, but so are experiences in which we have committed no sins.

Many priests know about Step Five, and Catholics who want to combine the Fifth Step with the sacrament of reconciliation should ask their priest for a special conference. The Fifth Step can take several hours, and this, of course, is much more time than a priest can spend with one person in confession. Combining Step Five with sacramental reconciliation is an ideal situation, for the Step Five counselor has no authority to forgive sins. The priest does, and I saw many young people yearning for this reassurance. My practice was to tell Catholics to follow up their Fifth Step with sacramental reconciliation, recounting those parts of their story where they felt a need for God's forgiveness.

Taking the Fifth Step

In summary, Step Five is an opportunity to share what you learned about yourself in Step Four. First, you read your inventory to God in a prayerful context. Next, you make an appointment to share this inventory with another human being — preferably someone with experience in hearing Fifth Steps. Allow at least two hours for your conference. Know that it is normal to be nervous about doing this step.

When you meet your Fifth Step counselor, be ready to share your inventory. You may choose to do this by reading what you have written in doing your inventory. Many people shared their inventories with me by telling me their life stories. Either way is fine. The main thing is to be totally honest about what your life has been like. Leave nothing out! Don't worry about upsetting your listener; most likely he or she has already heard it all. After doing Step Five, celebrate with some form of healthy enjoyment. Treat yourself and a loved one to a movie or a nice dinner. "You were lost but now are found." This calls for a party — at least that's how the father of the prodigal son in the gospel saw things.

This is not the end, of course. The Twelve Steps are not a one-time climb. It is recommended that you do a Fourth and Fifth

Step every year or so. The second time won't be as emotional as the first, but it will give you added insights into your life. So will the third, fourth, and so on. And to keep yourself in the reassurance of God's forgiving love, go to confession frequently.

Questions for Reflection

1. What makes it difficult for you to really let another person know your deepest thoughts and feelings? How can you overcome this difficulty?
2. What kind of masks and defenses do you use most often to hide your true feelings? (Example: humor, intellectualizing, silence, timidity, a "got-it-all-together" attitude, and so forth.)
3. How has your understanding of the sacrament of reconciliation (penance) changed through the years?
4. How do you feel about doing a Fifth Step as outlined in this chapter? What do you think you might gain from this step?

CHAPTER SIX

Eliminating Character Defects

STEP SIX

**Were entirely ready to have God
remove all these defects of character.**

The people who put together the Twelve Step program of Alcoholics Anonymous learned that it was emotional pain that fueled the compulsion to drink. By working the first five steps, they began to move out of emotional pain. Later, we shall see how Steps Eight and Nine enable the healing process to deepen.

After some degree of relief from pain has been experienced, however, the issue becomes how to *stay out of pain*. This is where Steps Six and Seven come in. These two steps address the issue of defects of character, which are at the root of our emotional pain. It is because of defects of character that we actually produce emotional pain in our minds. This is true for everyone, not only alcoholics. If we want to be free from emotional pain and the self-centeredness that accompanies it, we must eliminate our defects of character.

Understanding Emotional Pain

It is important that we have a clear understanding of the nature of emotional pain. We all experience pain in life. Birth, sickness, hunger, thirst, and death are all pains experienced in the physical realm. Natural pains experienced in the psychological realm are grief, guilt, hurt, and disappointment. These pains result from the feelings we have when certain discomforting situations arise.

We can handle our pain in two different ways. We can live through it gracefully, in which case the pain is resolved and we grow because of it; or we can fail to deal with it, in which case pain becomes an emotion. Feelings are our response to situations confronting us *now;* emotions are old feelings that never got resolved. There are three poisonous emotions: resentment, shame, and fear.

For an example of how this works, let's suppose I am a child and my mother promises to take me to the park. Just as we start to leave, a friend of my mother's drops by and they spend the afternoon visiting and talking. We never do go to the park. I feel angry and disappointed. When I show these feelings, however, I am told to stop being selfish. When my father comes home, I am scolded again for having been so impatient. I never get to resolve my anger about not going to the park.

What happens to my anger? It doesn't go away. I just push it down inside. Old anger that never gets resolved becomes resentment — an emotional poison held in the tissues of the body that affects my health. The next time I get mad in a similar situation, I experience both the situational feeling and the old emotion. My level of response is disproportionate to the situation. I become emotional.

Shame is the emotional conviction that "I'm no good." We all experience it in certain situations, but as with anger, if the shame is not resolved, it becomes poisonous. Likewise, fear experienced but not resolved becomes an emotion.

Because we live in an imperfect world of conditional love, everyone carries some intensity of resentment, shame, and fear. The more conditional love, abuse, and neglect we experience, the more shame, resentment, and fear we carry within us. This is common but not natural.

Identifying Character Defects

Emotional pain leaves us feeling we are "not okay" inside. The feeling part of our nature tells us something is wrong, and that something is *us!* This is an intolerable situation for the mind to endure. Something must be done to right this wrong. The intellectual part of our nature takes up the challenge and attempts to right the wrong by reversing its cause. Since the wrong is thought to be us, however, the project we undertake must be one of "making us okay." Thus the feeling attitude "I'm not okay" becomes balanced by the intellectual attitude "But I will be okay when...."

Actually, there is a sense in which the very statement "I'll be okay when..." is in itself the ultimate defect of character. "I'll be okay when..." implies the intellectual conclusion "I'm not okay," which is a false conclusion. The correct conclusion is "I don't *feel* okay," which is quite different from not *being* okay. "I feel" is a statement about my present situation, which presumably can change. "I am" refers to my existential situation, which is much harder to change. Of course, the young mind has not yet made a distinction between "I feel" and "I am."

The attitude "I'll be okay when..." places my happiness in a future that doesn't even exist. Only "now" exists. If I'm not okay now, I'll never be okay, for the future will be just another now that "I'll be okay when…" forbids me to experience. Furthermore, "I'll be okay when…" is a dynamic in which the goal keeps being reset. If I have been trying to make myself okay by losing twenty pounds and I finally succeed in doing it, "I'll be okay when…" just resets to another goal. Now I need to lose twenty more pounds — and maybe get a new job and a savings account to be okay.

There are several common ways in which people try to make themselves okay.

- "I'll be okay when…I'm in control" (meaning when I don't experience or demonstrate painful feelings).
- "I'll be okay when…other people approve of me — or are impressed with me."
- "I'll be okay when…I'm perfect" (meaning I no longer make mistakes).
- "I'll be okay when…I don't need others" (so they can't hurt me).

Control, approval, perfectionism, and autonomy are the four character defects most commonly observed. We believe that attaining these pseudo-values will make us okay — but, of course, they won't.

It is impossible to be in control, approved, perfect, and autonomous. None of these pseudo-values can be realized all the time because they are distortions of our nature. In trying to make ourselves okay by being in control, approved, perfect, and autonomous, we continue to generate fear, shame, and resentment. These, in turn, compel us toward the use of fixes such as alcohol, overeating, shopping binges, and so on.

In our efforts to attain control, approval, perfection, and autonomy, we frequently find ourselves comparing our successes and failures with those of others. This attitude is inherently judgmental. Toward people who seem to have more control, approval, perfection, and autonomy, we feel envy, jealousy, and hate. Toward those who are not doing as well as we are, we feel superior, self-justified, and righteous. If, in comparing ourselves with others, we find we are far behind, we may just give up and become lazy, procrastinating, and irresponsible. All these negative emotional attitudes reinforce a distorted self-image and keep us locked in patterns of emotional pain.

It is a shock to people when they discover that it is not life that is giving them shame, fear, and resentment, but that they are doing it to themselves. It is the way we react to life with our judgment and interminable "I'll be okay when..." that keeps us stuck in pain.

Of course, we would never willingly put ourselves into the rat race of trying to become okay if we knew we already were okay. We would not continue to generate and recycle our emotional pain if we knew how to resolve it.

Twelve Step programs make a nice distinction between blame and responsibility. It is not our fault we were conditioned to react to life as we do, so we cannot blame ourselves for being judgmental and attached to "becoming okay" through self-defeating strategies. On the other hand, all this blaming and judgment is going on in our minds, and we are responsible for our actions. Without judging ourselves as bad, dumb, and stupid for getting caught up in defects of character, we accept responsibility for changing our self-defeating attitudes.

We do so by affirming to ourselves the good news — God loves us *just as we are.* Everything God has created is okay — indeed, very good! Therefore, we are already okay. If we are already okay, there is no need to be caught up in trying to become okay. Nor is there any need to compare ourselves with others, because they are okay too.

Of course, we might not feel okay inside, but that's another matter. Not feeling okay is very different from not being okay. We do not identify being okay with how we feel, because we are more than how we feel. In fact, our emotional experience begins to stabilize as soon as we quit identifying ourselves with it. We are not our feelings — we *have* feelings.

Some may wonder how all this talk of already being okay squares with the doctrine of original sin. The Catholic view maintains that human nature is basically good but has become distorted in its ability to give and receive love. The redemption brought by Christ does not make bad people into good people, but it does enable us to love as he loves — in the Spirit.

Time for Change

Step Six says we must be *entirely ready* to drop our defects of character. We must want to be totally free of all this senseless effort to become okay through control, perfection, approval, and autonomy. We must want to be done with the insanity of constantly comparing ourselves with others and judging according to the results. We must want to be free of all this so we can be here now in love, which is of the essence of spirituality.

Not everyone is entirely ready to give up this miserable head trip, however. Many are still receiving some kind of payoff from their defects of character. To be completely free, we must also give up these payoffs, and many are unwilling to do so. In general, people do not drop their defects until the pain they produce exceeds the payoffs they harvest.

Of course, we don't have to wait until this tragic situation comes to pass. We can begin paying attention to how we are caught up in "I'll be okay when…." We can see how this mistaken notion robs us of the now and has us constantly striving to reach impossible goals.

Once we see this, we will probably be ready to change. Only then will the next step — Step Seven — bring lasting relief.

Questions for Reflection

1. "I'll be okay when…." What are some of the ways you have experienced this kind of drive?
2. Do you believe it is possible to be healed of fear, shame, and resentment? Why or why not?
3. What kinds of payoffs have you been receiving from your defects of character? Are you entirely ready to give these up?
4. God loves you just the way you are: do you believe this? What makes it hard to believe?

CHAPTER SEVEN

Letting Go, Letting God

STEP SEVEN

**Humbly asked Him to remove
our shortcomings.**

An old, somewhat irreverent story is told about a priest who went for a walk each day. In the course of this daily walk, he passed a mansion with a beautifully landscaped front lawn.

"What a beautiful lawn the Lord has grown!" the priest would shout to the gardener each morning. The gardener, who was always working on the grounds, would merely nod appreciatively in reply.

This went on for weeks and months. Finally the gardener, who was not a religious man, could take it no longer. The next time the priest came by and shouted, "What a beautiful lawn the Lord has grown!" the gardener answered, "It's a beautiful lawn, all right, Father, but you should have seen it when the Lord was taking care of it by himself!"

The gardener makes a good point. As with the garden of the mansion, nothing will happen in the garden of the soul unless we ourselves do some cultivating, planting, hoeing, and weeding.

In spite of this, we must humbly admit that much happens that is beyond our control. The gardener cannot take credit for the beauty of the flowers that adorn his lawn. This beauty is God's gift. The gardener simply helps to bring the beauty forth. So, too, the beauty unique to each person is a gift. Our spiritual work does not create this beauty; we only help it to come forth.

In Step Six, we identified our attachments to control, perfection, approval, and self-sufficiency as ways of trying to make ourselves okay. We saw that ultimately each of these attachments is unattainable, leaving us with a deep sense of not being okay. Attachments set us up for conditional happiness. As a result of working Step Six and realizing these truths about attachments, we became ready to lead a different life.

At first, Step Seven seems to suggest a magical solution to the problem of defects of character: just pray about them, and God will take them away. Prayer is needed, to be sure. Having recognized the depth of our entanglement with attachments, we do need to ask God's help to let go. But we must also do some of the work.

False Ego Needs

To begin meeting our true needs, we must stop indulging in behavior oriented toward approval, control, perfectionism, and self-sufficiency. Here are a few examples of such behavior.

1. *Approval.* Doing things to impress people; trying not to upset people (even when they need to be upset); doing things to please people, even if it goes against our values.

2. *Perfectionism.* Judging ourselves and others harshly because we or they make mistakes; procrastinating about something because we're afraid it might not come out right.

3. *Control.* Checking up on people; nagging; not letting others know our vulnerability; not letting others be themselves.

4. *Self-sufficiency.* Refusing to ask for help from others; striving for total security.

To work Step Seven, we have to give up these behaviors. When we find ourselves thinking about them, we check our thoughts, check our will, and decide to act differently.

But how do we act differently? What can we do?

To illustrate this point, I offer the story of two Zen students and their masters. The first student, a beginner, bragged, "My master is so powerful that I can hold up a sheet and he can project his image onto it from a distance." Unimpressed, the second student, a veteran, replied, "My master is so powerful that when he is hungry, he eats and when he is sleepy, he rests."

Defects of character are like that: they are attempts to project a certain image of ourselves. To meet our true needs, we must give up such craziness.

What are our true needs? It's a sign of our *dis*-ease that we often don't even know the answer to that question. Plants and animals in nature know their needs; only humans do not. As Mark Twain put it, "Man is the only animal that blushes. Or needs to."

True Needs

If we are able to renounce false needs, what is left will be true. False needs are the "fixes" we discussed in Step One and the defects of character listed above. Fixes are not true needs; they are addictive needs. Defects of character are not true needs; they are ego needs.

After making a decision to stop indulging in behaviors that support our defects of character, we do the following with regard to each one.

1. *Approval.* We realize we do not need the approval of others. We are loved by God just as we are. There is no need for others to let us know we are okay. *Our true need is for awareness of God's unconditional love for us.*

2. *Perfection.* We realize it is human to make mistakes; it is not a sin. We give ourselves permission to make mistakes. *Our true need is to do the best we can at whatever we do, knowing that we will make mistakes — and that it's okay.*

3. *Control.* We recognize that we control nothing but our attitude about what is happening. *Our true need is not to be in control but to be here-now-in-love.* This means a willingness to give and to receive, to be strong and vulnerable, to be authentic, not phony.

4. *Self-sufficiency.* We realize it's okay to depend on others. *Our true need is to provide prudently for our needs, knowing it's okay to ask for help when we need it.*

After letting go of false needs associated with approval, control, perfection, and self-sufficiency, we begin to discover our true needs. If we do not let go, even such basic needs as food, clothing, and shelter will be distorted by our defects. Letting go brings us to a more peaceful experience of our needs.

Tending the Garden

In working toward our spiritual growth, we may reach a point where we begin to wonder which things are God's responsibility and which are our own. We know that it is God who grows the garden, but we also know that, as his gardeners, we are the ones who must tend it.

Saint Ignatius of Loyola wrote, "Pray as if everything depends on God and work as if everything depends on you." Twelve

Step groups have adopted a similar piece of advice in the Serenity Prayer. This beautiful prayer [see Appendix One] helps us to identify the work we must do and to trust God to do the rest.

God, grant me the serenity to accept the things I cannot change.... What are the chief causes of my anxieties? Do I have any control over these people, things, circumstances? Am I willing to let go of what I cannot control?

The courage to change the things I can.... What do I control? What can I do about my situation? I can always control my attitude, the way I relate to people, places, things, circumstances. How do I need to change my attitude?

And the wisdom to know the difference.... Knowing what is my business, what is the other person's business, and what is God's business is hard. If I cannot change something, I need to let it go. I ask God's help to do so in trust.

Living one day at a time, enjoying one moment at a time.... Am I now/here? If not, I am no/where. I ask the grace to be attentive to the NOW in loving readiness.

Accepting hardships as the pathway to peace. Taking, as He did, this sinful world as it is, not as I would have it.... My cross is the burden that loving commitment has brought me. Do I accept my crosses? Do I see how rejecting them makes me and others miserable? Do I know that crosses lead to growth?

Trusting that He will make all things right if I surrender to His will... Do I trust God to care for things if I let go of control? Have I yet learned that his plans for me are best? Do I believe that in his will is my happiness? I ask for growth in faith.

*That I may be reasonably happy in this life...*Happiness is a consequence of living here-now-in-love. Am I unconditionally happy? Who do I blame for my unhappiness? Do I see that it is the way I react to life that causes happiness and unhappiness? I ask the grace to take responsibility for my own happiness.

And supremely happy with Him forever.... "The sufferings of this present time are as nothing compared with the glory to be revealed for us" (Romans 8:18). Do I cling to this life? Do I fear death? Does the prospect of heaven give me hope and joy? I ask for the grace to be hopeful.

Questions for Reflection

1. What are your true needs? How do these differ from false needs?
2. Of the four false ego needs listed in this chapter, which one is hardest for you to break free from? What does this chapter teach you about letting go?
3. How do you distinguish between what is your responsibility to change and what is God's responsibility to change? What are some of your struggles in letting go of what is not yours, but God's? Give an example.

CHAPTER EIGHT

Making Peace in Relationships

STEP EIGHT

**Made a list of all persons we had harmed,
and became willing to make amends to them all.**

Most of us have heard it said that a relationship is a two-way street, requiring give-and-take from both parties. There is a sense, however, in which a relationship is a one-way street. By this I mean a relationship consists of the thoughts, feelings, and memories we experience toward or about someone or something. Anytime we have thoughts, feelings, and memories toward or about someone or something, we have a relationship — even if that someone or something knows nothing about it and makes no response.

Think about how you still feel related to loved ones who have died. Surely, they are not reciprocating in any way that you can see, but this does not take away your thoughts, feelings, and memories of them and your sense of being connected with them. Think about a baseball or football team you follow. This, too, is a relationship. You might even have strong feelings about the success or failure of this team, even though the team knows nothing about your feelings.

You might be surprised to discover you have relationships going with people you never talk to, maybe even with pets, plants, and inanimate objects. For example, addiction counselors say that the alcoholic has a sick relationship with alcohol, preferring this inanimate object to healthy relationships with people.

This view of relationships as a one-way street means you carry relationships around in your head. In fact, your very experience of self comes from these relationships.

Who are you? You are the one who is in all these relationships. How you perceive yourself in relationships and how you imagine others perceiving you — this is largely the content of your own view of yourself, your self-image.

Obviously, there is room in the area of relationships for a tremendous amount of self-delusion. For example, how do you know that the attitude you imagine others have toward you is, in fact, their true position? And how do you know that your own view of the other is an accurate perception? So often we relate to who we think people are rather than who they really are. In addition to having a self-image or self-concept (your ideas about yourself), you have other-images and other-concepts. How do you know that in relating to other people you are not just relating to an idea about them that you have created?

The same can be asked about your relationship with God. Do you relate to the mysterious Yahweh who has no image or to some concept of God you have fabricated out of the culture? In the end, your concepts and ideas about God are the means by which you approach the mystery of God. God is beyond all definitions and concepts; however, you need these concepts to begin to understand how he acts. Concepts about God are necessary even to knowing that God is infinitely more than our concepts.

The foregoing reflection is not meant to be a clever demonstration of the human capacity for self-delusion. Rather, it is a starting point for true reconciliation in relationships and a healthier self-knowledge. If relationships — even active ones — are one-way streets, the first thing to do is to examine your own thoughts, feelings, and memories. Step Eight invites you to do this examination of all your relationships, especially those in which your thoughts, feelings, and memories bring guilt, shame, and resentment.

When you experience guilt, shame, and resentment in a relationship, you are not free. You are probably defensive and your guard is constantly up. You may also spend a good deal of time thinking about the relationship, carrying on imaginary conversations with this person, or fantasizing scenarios you may even act out one day. If the pain is very strong, you might spend a great deal of energy trying *not* to think about the relationship. These activities are often the cause of depression.

The real victim of guilt, shame, and resentment is the person who carries the pain. Even if the behavior of the other was positively immoral, the satisfaction of pronouncing moral judgment on that person's behavior does not erase the consequences of your own loss of inner freedom. If you desire to be truly free, you will recognize the importance of looking honestly at where you are in your relationships. Step Eight is about "taking a look." Step Nine is the follow-up, where you will actually do something to help make amends or reconciliation.

Make a List

Step Eight invites you to make a list of all persons you have harmed. This is the best place to start. Of course, you do not always know if you actually have harmed others, but frequently there is no doubt about it. Even if you only *think* you may have harmed someone, put it down on the list.

1. Name of the other person.
2. What I did (behavior, not motives) that I think (or know) hurt this person.
3. How I feel about my behavior.
4. What I think the other felt and suffered because of my behavior.
5. How this has affected our relationship.

Take your time. Be thorough and honest with yourself. At this point, you do not have to do anything with the information you are putting on your list. Simply compile the list as thoroughly and honestly as possible. In Step Nine, you will decide what to do with this information. Needless to say, you should be careful where you put your list, for it is extremely personal and confidential information.

Taking responsibility for the wrongs you have done to others is really all that Step Eight asks you to do. But because a relationship is also your thoughts, feelings, and memories about how others have treated you, it is important that your Step Eight list includes those considerations as well. Many times, guilt, shame, and resentment have more to do with the behavior of others toward you than yours toward them. This is especially true for those who suffered abuse while growing up. Here are suggestions for a second list.

1. Name of the other person.
2. What this person did (behavior, not motives) that hurt me.

3. How I feel about this behavior.
4. What I have suffered because of this behavior.
5. How this has affected our relationship.

Note that in both lists you are advised to focus on behavior and not motives. This is all that is necessary. You are not required to deal with your motives nor the motives of others. For one thing, you do not always even know what they are.

You are also asked about feelings. Do not confuse this with motives. Do not say, "I felt it was uncaring for her to break her promise." This is a judgment of motives. Instead say, "I felt hurt and angry when she broke her promise." This is more honest.

Be Willing to Make Amends

Making these lists will take considerable time and is likely to be painful. Your actions should be motivated by a willingness to make amends. This implies a desire on your part to get straight in all your relationships. It also implies your desire to be free from the slavery of shame, guilt, and resentment. Because you want to be free inside yourself, you are willing to examine your relationships — your thoughts, feelings, and memories toward others.

The desire to be free leads to humility. Undoubtedly, your list will include behavior you are not proud of — in fact, you may be downright ashamed. If you can see that this shame is a poison in your soul, then you become willing to put away false pride so you can get the poison out. Most false pride is a compensation for inner shame, but true humility is the death of false pride.

Finally, we note that a willingness to make amends is itself a movement of love. What is this willingness but love's own movement toward reconciliation and unity? In short, the willingness to make amends is evidence of the presence of the Holy

Spirit. When we are alive in the Spirit, we experience serenity and joy even while we make unpleasant lists.

Questions for Reflection

1. What is harder for you: to forgive others or to ask for forgiveness? Why?
2. Why is it important to leave blame and motives out of a confrontation with others?
3. What is the difference between guilt and shame? What are the consequences of each?
4. Why is it important to "clear the slate" in all your relationships? What happens if you do not do this?

CHAPTER NINE

Making Amends and Forgiveness

STEP NINE

Made direct amends to such people wherever possible, except when to do so would injure them or others.

An old saying has it that if we want to know where we stand with God, we must look first at the quality of our human relationships. "Whoever says he is in the light, yet hates his brother, is still in the darkness. Whoever loves his brother remains in the light, and there is nothing in him to cause a fall" (1 John 2:9-10).

In Step Eight, we made a list of persons we had harmed and became willing to make amends. We acknowledged the importance of listing persons who had harmed us, and we became willing to forgive them. Considering Saint John's teaching on relationships, light, and darkness, we see that making amends and forgiving is a way of coming into the light. Withholding forgiveness and refusing to make amends result in our remaining in darkness.

We can't experience true spiritual light at the expense of human relationships. "If you bring your gift to the altar, and there recall that your brother has anything against you, leave your gift there at the altar, go first and be reconciled with your brother, and then come and offer your gift. Settle with your opponent quickly while on the way to court with him" (Matthew 5:23-25). Strong words to be sure — and from the Lord himself! In Step Nine, we obviously have a very important spiritual principle.

Making amends has to do with the wrongs we have done to others. We must deal with this first. What did we do that hurt others? What did we fail to do that we should have done? How has this resulted in hurt for others? For us? Step Eight invited us to reflect honestly on these questions. Step Nine invites us to act upon this information.

Step Nine presupposes a willingness to go to any length to get straight in our human relationships. There is one qualifier, however. We must consider the probable consequences of our efforts. Will they cause problems for others? Honesty in a relationship is important, but love must prevail.

Marital infidelity is one example of an injustice it is best not to bring up. If we've been unfaithful but are now "turning over a new leaf," the best way to make amends is to be faithful, committed, and loving. Sharing a past infidelity with one's spouse might be honest, but the consequences in terms of hurt and lost trust can be devastating. I have seen marriages destroyed because of a careless working of Step Nine.

It is quite another matter, however, when a spouse already knows about the infidelity. Then the thing to do is be honest and pledge fidelity in the future. Even then, trust will have to be regained.

There are other times when it is wise to let the past alone. It's important to remember that while making amends does require that we do something to correct injustices we have perpetrated, it does not require that others know about it — especially if the knowledge will be hurtful.

Approaching Others

Of course, in some circumstances, words are important. Sometimes when we have hurt another and that person knows about it, false pride discourages us from making amends. It doesn't matter if what we did was unintentional. If we have hurt someone, we need to make amends — for the sake of our own peace of mind. We need to exchange words with the other person in a letter, a phone call, or a personal visit. It is important to plan what we will say and how we will say it. Sometimes it helps to review our plan with a third person, especially if it involves a phone call or a personal visit.

In making amends, the importance of speaking from our Step Eight list cannot be overstated. We should talk about what we have done, how the other has been hurt, and how it has affected the relationship.

A few years ago, *Newsweek* ran an open letter from an adult child of an alcoholic to his father. The older man had recently been through a treatment program for his addiction. In his enthusiasm for recovery, he went to his son to make amends. What he said was something like this: "Son, I know we had hard times, and I know you were hurt by some of the things I did. For anything I might have done that might have hurt you, I'm sorry." In his open letter, the son objected that this was too easy and cheap — and he was absolutely correct.

After doing a thorough Step Eight, the father should have been specific: "Son, I'm getting my life straightened out, and I need to talk to you about what it's been like between us. Remember the time I told you I'd take you fishing and you got up early, made us breakfast, packed a lunch, and waited? When you finally came to wake me up, I told you to get the hell out of my room. I know you were hurt by that. I've felt bad about it ever since...." Get the idea? To really clear the air, we must acknowledge specific deeds and the feelings we have about these deeds.

Oh, yes — it will hurt! We might even cry. But that's all right. We're already hurting from these broken relationships. It was the avoidance of this sort of necessary suffering that caused us to get so psychologically sick.

We must be prepared to face another possibility. The person with whom we need to make amends may not forgive us. That outcome is out of our control. All we can do is acknowledge what happened, apologize (and say "I apologize," not "I'm sorry"), and offer to make restitution if that is called for. Sometimes the other person is angry and rejects our attempts to make amends at first but later accepts. At any rate, there is nothing we can do to control the responses of others.

What happens if a person with whom we need to make amends has already died? I suggest writing this person a letter, then reading it aloud, perhaps at the grave site on All Souls' Day or on the anniversary of the person's death. After reading the letter, burn it or leave it as an offering with the flowers at the grave. If this graveside visitation is not feasible, we can do it in church or at home.

Forgiveness

Everything that has been said about making amends also applies to forgiveness. We have to make a list, consider the consequences of sharing it with the person who has hurt us, choose the appropriate means of doing so, then be specific about deeds and feelings. If the other person gets upset, we must allow him or her the right to these feelings — even the right to reject our approach

— and explain that we are working at letting go of our anger and resentment.

This is what it means to forgive — to let go of resentment. To forgive does not mean we have to agree with what the other person has done or forget what has happened. Neither does it mean we must continue to be in a relationship with that person. We may choose to have no relationship for a number of reasons. Forgiveness means letting go of resentment because resentment is bad for us, and we bring it into other relationships.

Recently I read in one of Dr. Susan Forward's best-selling books on relationships that it isn't necessary to forgive people, that we could have our anger toward them. This is only true to the extent that our anger does not turn into resentment. Resentment is anger turned into hatred. When we resent, we wish the other harm. This is in direct contrast to love, which "is not rude, it does not seek its own interests, it is not quick-tempered, it does not brood over injury" (1 Corinthians 13:5).

Sometimes our resentment toward another is so strong that we do not *want* to forgive. In that case, it helps to recall the old phrase, "To err is human, to forgive divine." When we are stuck in resentment, we must pray for the willingness to forgive. We don't have to approach the other until we're ready, but we can begin to forgive through prayer now. Praying for the well-being of the other is a powerful way to begin the process of forgiveness.

A resentful woman once told me she prayed to be able to see her husband as God saw him. "All of a sudden, while talking to my husband that night, I saw him for what he was: a man, just a confused, scared man trying hard to keep his life together and not having a clue about how to talk about it with me."

She wept as she said this. Her husband was not the ogre she had imagined but just a man. It's easy to forgive people their faults — especially since we happen to have faults of our own.

"Father, forgive them, they know not what they do," Jesus prayed from the cross (Luke 23:34). People who have hurt us are like that. They probably really didn't know what they did, or they wouldn't have done it. Years of family therapy have convinced me that most of the time people don't mean to hurt one another. It's just that they have all this anger from being mistreated through the years, and they don't know how to get rid of it. So they pass it on from generation to generation. It literally rolls on down through the centuries, even though no one wants it or intends to pass it on. How many people say they'll never be like their parents and then wind up treating their children the same way?

If we're honest in making amends, then we know how easy it is to hurt others and how it is usually unintended. It helps to give those who have hurt us the benefit of the doubt on this point. We hold them responsible for their behavior but do not judge their motives, for we just do not know what is going on in their hearts.

Finally, we give ourselves time to forgive. Typically, forgiveness is a process, not an event. For some it takes months, even years, to forgive. The healing process is out of our hands. All we can do is cultivate the willingness to forgive.

Promises of the Twelve Steps

During the last ten years, I have worked with hundreds of people in Twelve Step programs. In my own life, I see the Steps as a process for letting go and letting God. I can say with certainty that *they are hard work!* This Ninth Step in particular goes entirely against the ways of the world.

People become happy and serene to the extent that they work the Steps. Even in recovery groups, there are people who go to meetings but don't do the Steps. There are some who know a lot *about* the Steps but don't put them into practice. Only by working the Steps can we appreciate the light into which they lead us.

The "Big Book," *Alcoholics Anonymous,* acknowledges the tremendous courage it takes to do Steps Eight and Nine. Only a person who really wants to grow will do these two steps. I hope you do! In its discussion on Step Nine, *Alcoholics Anonymous* begins a reflection that has come to be known as "the promises of the program."

If we are painstaking about this phase of our development, we will be amazed before we are halfway through. We are going to know a new freedom and a new happiness. We will not regret the past nor wish to shut the door on it. We will comprehend the word *serenity* and we will know peace. No matter how far down the scale we have gone, we will see how our experience can benefit others. That feeling of uselessness and self-pity will disappear. We will lose interest in selfish things and gain interest in our fellows. Self-seeking will slip away. Our whole attitude and outlook on life will change. Fear of people and of economic security will leave us. We will know intuitively how to handle situations that used to baffle us. We will suddenly realize that God is doing for us what we could not do for ourselves.

Are these extravagant promises? We think not. They are being fulfilled among us — sometimes quickly, sometimes slowly. They will always materialize if we work for them.

Questions for Reflection

1. Why is it important to make amends when you have hurt another?
2. Why is it important to be specific in making amends?
3. How do you experience forgiveness: as an event or an ongoing process? Explain.
4. What is the sign of the presence of forgiveness? What is the sign of its absence?

CHAPTER TEN

Living One Day at a Time

STEP TEN

Continued to take personal inventory and when we were wrong promptly admitted it.

How to live one day at a time? How to keep little problems from becoming big problems? These are the concerns of Step Ten. The previous nine steps have focused on turning away from self-indulgence, centering in God, and dealing with the consequences of indulgence. The final three steps have to do with maintaining spiritual health in daily living. You might say that the first nine steps are a major housecleaning process, while the last three are about keeping the house clean.

As a result of working the first nine steps, we begin to experience inner freedom, serenity, and a sense of God's presence.

These are wonderful fruits, and we do not want to lose them. But neither do we want to continue going through the rather intense processes of reflection and reconciliation undertaken thus far. Steps Ten, Eleven, and Twelve round out the process, summarizing and reinforcing the growth we have gained so far.

Inventory and Amends

The language of Step Ten calls to mind Steps Four (made a searching and fearless moral inventory of ourselves), Five (admitted to God, to ourselves, and to another human being the exact nature of our wrongs), Eight (made a list of persons we had harmed and became willing to make amends), and Nine (made direct amends to such people wherever possible, except when to do so would injure them or others).

If you have worked these steps, you know the benefits they bring. You also know they required a great deal of soul-searching and risk-taking. As a result of this work, however, you are breaking free from the limiting influences of the past. Old feelings of guilt, shame, resentment, and fear have been relieved. The slate of emotional pain has been wiped clean, making it possible for new levels of peace and growth to develop.

By working Step Ten daily, you can keep the slate clean. Like Steps Four and Five, Ten calls for daily inventory; like Steps Eight and Nine, Ten calls for making amends where necessary. In a sense then, Step Ten is a recapitulation of those four steps, but on a daily basis, dealing with issues of that day only rather than with your whole life.

There are many ways to do a daily inventory. The first and best is to live each moment in awareness. Too many people go through life not quite awake and not quite asleep — just putting in time. As Thoreau wrote, most people lead lives of "quiet desperation." This attitude is the antithesis of spiritual living! Old behaviors return quickly in such a state of mind.

Living in awareness calls for being present to what you are doing, to your inner life. Gently keep your attention in the now, doing what you're doing, open to your feelings, willing to give of yourself as needed, and enjoying the sights and sounds around you. This is a difficult practice — the hardest you will ever do. But it is the healthiest of attitudes and the one most likely to keep you from slipping back into old habits.

Living in awareness is an ongoing inventory. Open to your feelings and honestly monitoring your motives, you stay in touch with your inner life through the day. If a selfish motive arises, you recognize it, call it by name, and then get back into being here-now-in-love. If you slip into old habits — for example, you speak harshly to another — you acknowledge it to yourself as soon as possible, then go to the person and make amends.

This is Step Ten in a nutshell — self-honesty and making amends when you hurt another. Working this step is a lifelong process. The fruit of living in awareness is that unhealthy habits of thought and feeling eventually drop away. An old axiom says, "If you don't use it, you lose it." This is as true of unhealthy behavior as of other habits. If your attention is in the now, you are not being anxious about the future or concerned with the past — preoccupations that drain away psychic energy. Coming into the now, the moment of God, increases your energy.

Eventually, living in the now will free your attention from disquietude, but this takes time. Meanwhile, the best discipline is to notice where your attention is and gently focus in the now whenever thoughts start to stray into the future or the past.

Another way to work Step Ten is to take time for daily examen of consciousness. Many Catholics have heard of the examination of conscience, but for daily life, the examen is more effective in maintaining one in spiritual health. Set aside fifteen to twenty minutes at the end of the day for prayer and review of your day. A suggested format is described on the next page.

1. Take a few moments of quiet. Breathe deeply. Ask God to help you see yourself as you truly were during the day.
2. Look back over your day — not to see what you did wrong but to honestly acknowledge what was going on with you and others.

   - What happened? What did I do today?
   - How did I feel? Why did I feel that way?
   - Were my expectations and beliefs reasonable?

3. Affirm the healthy things you recognize.
4. Admit to yourself and God the unhealthy things. Ask God's forgiveness, believe it is yours, then decide if you need to apologize or make amends.
5. Use creative visualization to grow stronger. Honestly acknowledge the troubling situations of the day. See and feel yourself acting honestly and lovingly in these situations. Ask God for the grace to help you act in this new way.
6. Close with simple awareness of the sights and sounds around you, grateful for the good things in your life.

This process can be undertaken as a daily journal exercise or by prayerfully reviewing your day in your own mind. I like to take a walk before bedtime for examen. The important thing is to do it. It is a discipline, to be sure, but a very important one.

Tremendous spiritual rewards come from the examen. You will grow in self-knowledge and find it easier to live in awareness. By settling your mind at bedtime, you will sleep more peacefully. You will continue to break free from old reactions and gain power to choose your response to situations.

Saint Ignatius of Loyola is reported to have said that given a choice between daily prayer and examen, he would choose the examen. If that's how this great saint saw things, then surely we should make the examen a daily practice.

Commitment to Growth

At this point in the Twelve Step process, it is worthwhile to review your commitment to growth. Living in awareness, daily examen, and the disciplines of Steps Eleven and Twelve require a commitment of time and practice.

It has been said that most people do not want to grow — they only want to stop hurting. Steps One through Nine bring relief from old hurts and enable us to begin waking up. Staying awake is another matter. Staying awake means beginning to discover the deeper, more mysterious dimensions of your own nature, your union with God, and your oneness with all of creation.

The idea of living life fully awake frightens many people. Having experienced relief from pain, they become complacent, backing away from the call to grow. They cling to their old self-image, preferring it to the true, mysterious levels of personhood beginning to emerge. As Saint Teresa of Avila stated many times, the spiritual journey requires a courageous response. To let go of the known and move into the unknown is frightening. You will need to go back to Step Two again and again, reaffirming your hope in Christ as the basis of your courage to keep going.

Those who respond to the call to grow will experience life to the full, just as Jesus promised in the Gospel of John.

Questions for Reflection

1. What makes it difficult for you to be here-now-in-love? How do you disturb yourself out of the present moment?
2. How committed are you to growth? Are you willing to "go to any length" to follow the Lord Jesus? Explain.

3. Share some of the struggles and benefits you have come to know as a result of doing the awareness exam described in this chapter.
4. "Easy does it." "Live one day at a time." "Do what you're doing." "Progress, not perfection." "Let go and let God." How do these slogans help you to stay focused?

CHAPTER ELEVEN

Meeting God Through Prayer

STEP ELEVEN

Sought through prayer and meditation to improve our conscious contact with God *as we understood Him,* praying only for knowledge of His will for us and the power to carry that out.

Christianity is unique in that it invites us into a love relationship with God. This relationship is personal, for love is personal and the incarnate Son of God is a person, Jesus Christ, who loves us. No other world religion invites one to know God in this way, for it is only through the revelation of Jesus that we learn of the loving nature of the transcendent God. For Jesus, knowing God and loving God mean the same thing.

Knowing and loving God is precisely what we need to be

happy. There is no happiness in living only for self, and living for others easily turns into codependency. Our hearts desire more than this, for our hearts were created to know God's love. We all have a desire for greater meaning in life than the world holds out for us — and only God can satisfy this desire.

Because love is neither an object the senses can observe nor a mere concept for the mind to know, it is impossible to define. As the very essence of God, love is the ultimate mystery.

And yet we know somehow that love is real. We know when we are loved by another, and we know when we are not. Even if love brings us to suffering — as it sometimes does — it also brings us to greater life. Life and love are connected: "No one has greater love than this, to lay down one's life for one's friends" (John 15:13). Love is giving life, and life is the creative movement of love.

Another thing we know is that love is experienced in the context of relationship. As the creative movement and expression of life itself, love can only happen "between two" in relationship. This manner of relating is of a special kind in which we are not just looking to "get something" from another but are willing also to give of ourselves. There must be openness, listening, risk, trust, and vulnerability on both sides if love is to take root within us. Jesus invites us into such a relationship. He asks for our openness, trust, and vulnerability. He himself is open, trusting, and vulnerable. When we fail to love, Jesus is also forgiving, inviting us to make amends, put the past behind us, and start over again.

Relationship With God

It follows, then, that the way to know God's personal love is to be in relationship with God. This is different from merely believing in God. It is possible to believe in God — even to be a brilliant and orthodox theologian — without being in a relationship of love.

It is the same way with people. It is possible to know certain people and to learn about them from their family members, even to admire them from a distance. But until we relate to them ourselves, we do not have a personal relationship with them.

Other examples of lack of relationship are the people in our lives to whom we were once close but from whom we now feel distanced. Is it because we have stopped relating to them? Husbands and wives know that if they do not take time to relate to each other, they lose their sense of love for each other.

It is the same way with God. If we want to really know and love God, we must spend time on the relationship. We can do this throughout the day by including God in our thinking and decision-making and listening as God speaks to us in our consciences. This is prayer.

But for this ongoing awareness of God's presence to grow, we must take time to be alone with God in a formal manner of relating. A happily married couple must not only be communicative and considerate of each other through the day but also take special time to talk about their deeper thoughts and feelings. So it is in our relationship with God.

Essentials of Prayer

Once we see prayer in terms of relationship, the traditional teachings about prayer and the message of Step Eleven begin to make sense. Consider the following disciplines and suggestions, found in many books on prayer, in terms of their contribution to our growth in relationship with God.

- *Commitment.* We make time for what is important to us.
  If growing in love and knowledge of God is important,
  our commitment to focus daily on that relationship is a
  must.

- *Time.* It takes time to get in touch with our deeper feelings and thoughts. It is good to set aside at least twenty to thirty minutes daily to relate to God.
- *Solitude.* Husbands and wives do not want interruptions when they are sharing intimate matters. In the same vein, Jesus says, "Go to your inner room, close the door, and pray to your Father in secret. And your Father who sees in secret will repay you" (Matthew 6:6).
- *Silence.* The proper posture is a great help in coming to silence. Sit comfortably, back straight, head slightly lowered. Gently follow your breath: breathe in God's love, allow distractions to fall away, and let go of anxieties as you breathe out.
- *Sacred Reading.* Select a short Scripture passage. Sacred reading is different from reading Scripture for content or study. During prayer we accept Scripture as a letter from our beloved and listen to the words as though spoken by a loved one.
- *Meditation.* How does the passage speak to us? What does it say about God? About our relationship with God? About our lifestyle? Such meditation on Scripture helps us to become attuned to God's Spirit at the level of thought.
- *Personal Response.* Sometimes called affective prayer because it concerns the feeling response we make to God. It is our time to express personal petitions, intercessions, thanksgiving, and remorse. If our feelings make it hard to quiet ourselves, we might do this before Sacred Reading. We pray for knowledge of God's will and power to carry it out: "Lord, what would you have me do today to help further your kingdom?"
- *Loving Silence.* It is good to be with God in silence. When lovers have said all they have to say to each other, they discover a bond deeper than words. So it is in

relationship with God. This is contemplative prayer, and eventually this type of prayer will become the mainstay of the relationship. In loving silence, we come to know not only Christ's love for us but his own love for the Father. This is the Holy Spirit, the living flame described by mystics — the love our hearts desire.

Contemplative Prayer Forms

There is much interest in contemplative prayer today, and rightly so. It is the deepest bond of love between a person and God. We are all called to know this level of union, but not all will experience it in the same way.

Most people who persevere in prayer as described above will experience contemplation as a natural outgrowth of their prayer. To further encourage the growth of contemplative prayer, some practice "centering prayer." In centering prayer, we follow the process above, reserving the last ten to fifteen minutes for simply being present to God in loving silence. We use a prayer word like *Jesus* or *Abba* to focus on God when attention strays, letting go of the prayer word when the mind comes to peace. The practice is one of gently bringing our attention back to God again and again with the prayer word, then resting in loving silence at the level of will.

Another springboard to contemplation experienced by many Christians is the charismatic gift of tongues, or *glossolalia.* In glossolalia, an unintelligible babbling of praise arises from the depths. This praise is inspired by the Holy Spirit and brings about healing and serenity. Praying in tongues is a form of active contemplation, for it is the Spirit praying in the person. The person is free to stop the prayer at any time — we are not talking about any kind of possession. But giving the Spirit free rein to lead us to praise in tongues generally leads to a new depth of silence, when tongues cease and loving union remains.

I heartily recommend both centering prayer and charismatic prayer to anyone who desires to experience contemplation. It is best to undertake these practices in dialogue with an experienced spiritual director with knowledge of these prayer forms.

Change and Growth

It is impossible to be in a loving relationship without being changed in some way by it. In love, our better qualities rise to the surface and grow stronger. But as we take greater risks and become more vulnerable, some of the darker, hidden forces within also emerge.

This is a real time of testing in the relationship. What will we do when we begin to discover some of these unconscious energies? Will we project them onto others, as most people do, then react to them in the other? Or will we sit with them in our prayer, accepting them as our own, knowing that God has always known about these qualities but loved us anyway?

Working the Twelve Steps helps to heal many old hurts and to transform much darkness. Of all the steps, however, this one is the most important for going deeper and deeper into the realization of our relationship with God. This realization is the source of our healing and inner freedom.

When we spend time with a loved one, we take on some of their qualities. The same happens when we spend time with God. By taking time each day to deepen our relationship with God through prayer, we become more and more transformed into the person God intends for us to be. We become more godlike: loving, simple, free, fearless, wise, and compassionate. In becoming more godlike, we also become more truly human, expressing in our everyday life the best qualities of humanity. Finally, we become more ourselves, discovering the beautiful person God has created, a person who can only be fully revealed by God.

Questions for Reflection

1. How do you pray? Does your prayer help you become more aware of God's presence through the day?
2. Do you believe it is important to take regular time to be alone with God in prayer? Why or why not?
3. What are your views on charismatic prayer? Centering prayer? If you are not familiar with either of these forms, are you open to trying them? Why or why not?
4. What is your image of God's will? Do you see life as a drama, with God as the playwright and you as the actor who has to learn your part from God? Or do you envision an interpersonal, freedom-to-freedom relationship in which you and God dialogue and negotiate to discover what is right for you?
5. Do you believe that doing God's will is your happiness? Why or why not?

CHAPTER TWELVE

Walking the Walk

STEP TWELVE

Having had a spiritual awakening as the result of these Steps, we tried to carry this message [to others], and to practice these principles in all our affairs.

This step begins with an astonishing affirmation: it says that those who have worked Steps One through Eleven have had a spiritual awakening!

What does this mean?

The best response to this question is "Truly work Steps One through Eleven. Then no one will need to tell you what a spiritual awakening is, for you will have firsthand, experiential knowledge of what it means." That's the kind of knowledge the Twelve Steps invite you to discover.

It might be helpful at this point to distinguish between living a moral life and living a spiritual life. Morality refers to living according to principles that we recognize as good. For Christians, the Ten Commandments and the Laws of the Church are considered authoritative moral guidelines. When we keep these principles, there is greater order in our lives and more harmony in the community. For many — perhaps most — Christians, religion is understood in this way: as an invitation to lead a good and moral life and so gain the reward of heaven as a merit for good behavior when they die. There is no denying the value of a life lived according to moral principles. Would that all people were doing so! But this is not the meaning of spirituality. Spirituality takes us into the depths of ourselves, where we get in touch with our greatest motives, our brokenness, our sinfulness — our need for God. It is possible to live a moral life without entering very deeply into our inner life.

Yet we must recognize that there is no entering into the spiritual life without a sound moral life. When we violate our moral values, we experience guilt, shame, hurt, and other painful emotions that disturb the inner life. By living a moral life — being true to our values — we come to know a peace of conscience that allows us to begin to go within. So we see that moral living is not separate from spirituality but is, in fact, the foundation for the spiritual life. We might even go so far as to say that spirituality is living the moral life with an interior dimension — awake to the origin and meaning of the principles valued by conscience.

The Value of Spirituality

Two monks lived in the desert. One day, Brother Jacob went to see Abbot Simon about his monastic practice. "I have been keeping the Rule, but it seems there is something missing," said Brother Jacob. "What else is there?" Abbot Simon held up his hands and flames of fire emanated from his fingers. "You might also catch fire," he replied, inviting Brother Jacob into the spiritual journey.

This is similar to the story of Jesus and the rich young man. (See Mark 10:17-22.) The rich young man was living a good and moral life, but he was still unsatisfied. "What else is there?" he seemed to be asking Jesus. Jesus looked at him in love, then invited him to give up everything and become a disciple. The rich young man went away sad, however, for he was unwilling to give up his attachments for the sake of spirituality.

From these two stories, we learn that spirituality is about catching fire. It is about living life to the full, awake to God's presence within and outside of ourselves. As George Schemel, S.J., put it, spirituality brings

a more intense, integrated human experience. A deeper sensitivity to life in general; loves are more loving, sorrows are more sorrowful, angers are more angry. Truth is more compelling. Reality is more real. The interpersonal relationship with God and others is more challenging and occupying.

(Ignatian Spirituality and the Directed Retreat)

I believe our deepest, truest desire is to live a spiritual life. The human soul is a direct creation of God and yearns to know itself in relationship with God. Until we wake up to ourselves at this level of soul, we do not really know who we are, and we don't really know life to the full.

The problem, as the story of the rich young man illustrates, is that there is a resistance within us to this waking-up process. We are quite content to settle for less than the best and to resist the spiritual journey. We know the inner journey will require a confrontation with our pain and willfulness. It is no picnic, as anyone who has worked through the Twelve Steps has undoubtedly discovered.

The avoidance of pain accounts for most of our inordinate attachments and addictive fixes. In fact, we do well to recognize how hard we work to avoid dealing with our inner pain and brokenness. Even part of our endeavor to lead a moral life might issue from this avoidance — if we can only do the right things, then maybe we'll feel better inside. It works a little bit, but not much.

Christianity points the true way. To come to the risen life, we must first pick up our crosses and follow in the footsteps of Christ. We cannot go around the mess that lies within; we must go through it. But we do not go alone. Jesus is with us, showing us how to walk, reassuring us of forgiveness, pointing out the way. Many of us see the Twelve Steps as a means to help us carry this cross and walk this inner walk with Jesus. By using the Twelve Steps in this way, we come to deal with our pain within and restore a moral dimension to our lives. It is the genius of the Steps that the inner life and the moral dimension are dealt with simultaneously.

By working the Steps, we are healed, our conscience comes to peace, and we awaken to the reality of God's life within and about us. This awakening is the "pearl of great price" that Jesus spoke of and that Father Schemel described in the quote above. It is the abundant life we long for but have pursued in the past through erroneous attachments and fixes. So magnificent is this life that we know without a doubt, from our own experiences of it, that this is the way we must go from now on. Having come to taste the life of the Spirit, we know we cannot go back — not without great desolation of soul. Henceforth, our destiny is linked with Christ, and heaven is our true home.

Stages on the Spiritual Journey

At this point, I think it would be worthwhile to sketch in broad outlines what the Catholic mystical literature has to say about the spiritual journey. There is no doubt that the Twelve Steps introduce one to that journey, and that is good. But the literature of

Twelve Step groups reflects an understanding of only the very beginnings of the spiritual journey. More and more, however, there is talk of stages of recovery, with workshops and retreats springing up to develop these themes. So at least there is a recognition that the spiritual journey is a developmental process and not simply a single "awakening event."

Traditional mystical writers have described three stages of the spiritual journey: purgative, illuminative, and unitive. These stages taper off one into the other but ultimately describe the different kinds of issues and experiences encountered along the way. While other developmental theories focus on moral, social, cognitive, and other growth trajectories, the three stages of spiritual development are concerned with the degree of union with God that a person is able to sustain in daily living.

The three stages of spiritual growth are described below, using terms from the addiction-recovery movement.

A. *Purgative Stage:* Breaking With the Past. This stage takes at least one year.
   1. Giving up the most destructive fix/attachment/false center.
   2. Recentering life in God. Related to Steps Two, Three, and Eleven.
   3. Dealing with consequences of destructive fix/attachment/center.
      a. Restabilizing body systems (proper diet, exercise, sleep).
      b. Steps Four and Five.
      c. Steps Eight and Nine.
   4. Find "new playgrounds and playmates."
      — Dark Night of the Senses —

B. *Illuminative Stage:* Becoming Your True Self in Christ. This stage takes at least two years.

5. Giving up secondary fixes/attachments/false centers.
6. Deepening relationship with God.
   a. Step Two: education, spiritual reading.
   b. Step Three: surrender, lifestyle changes.
   c. Step Eleven: growing in prayer.
7. Dealing with consequences of secondary fixes/attachments/false centers.
   a. Steps Four and Five.
   b. Steps Eight and Nine.
   c. Step Ten.
8. Dealing with defects of character/unhealthy attitudes.
   a. Steps Six and Seven.
   b. Family of origin issues (can involve therapy).
9. Learning to meet true needs and to let go of false ego needs.
   a. True needs — food, shelter, clothing, sleep, exercise, play/fun/humor, honest relationships, choice/freedom, meaning, intellectual growth, aesthetic growth, prayer, creative expression.
   b. Falso ego needs — appreciation, recognition, control, approval, perpetuating a fixed identity, being "special."
10. Sharing the gift of recovery.
    a. Step Twelve.
    b. Service.

       — Dark Night of the Spirit —

C. *Unitive Stage:* Living in Union With God. This stage is ongoing.
   11. Giving up false identity attachments (Steps Six and Seven).
       a. Disidentifying with roles, labels, self-judgments, others' judgments (that is, self-image).
       b. Accepting, validating the beauty and mystery of the true self.

12. Deepening life of prayer (Step Eleven).
13. Simplifying lifestyle (Steps Three and Twelve).
14. Being here-now-in-love (Steps Ten and Twelve).

My experience in using the Twelve Steps in spiritual direction has been that the spiritual journey does indeed move along the lines sketched above. I have found, too, that the issues people are dealing with generally cluster around three or four adjacent points. For example, a person might be in touch with points 5 through 8 at any given time but not with issues much further down the line. Those issues will arise when the groundwork has been laid by doing the work prescribed in the earlier stages.

The above framework also demonstrates the place of the Steps in helping one to grow. In truth, we are never finished working the Twelve Steps. We only go deeper and deeper into their meaning and implications as we work them.

Finally, we note the "Nights of the Soul" between the Stages. These are times when the relationship between the conscious and unconscious dimensions are readjusting to accommodate a deepening union with God. During these times, we can feel as if we are not progressing but regressing. Aridities and times of emotional upheaval are common to those going through these Nights. Space does not permit a thorough treatment of them, but suffice it to say that there is a tremendous difference between the aridity of a Dark Night and the complacency resulting from spiritual neglect. Making such distinctions is one of the issues of spiritual direction, which anyone on the spiritual journey will discover to be of great value.

Giving and Receiving

Another genius of the Twelve Steps is that they do not en-courage one to "carry the message to others" until the first eleven

Steps have been worked. If we would invite others to experience the good news, we must ourselves be credible witnesses to its reality. Most of us have been turned off at one time or another by the proselytizing efforts of a recent convert to a spiritual movement or retreat. Our worst fear is that we will turn out to be a fanatic like that person seems to be.

Far more credible is the serenity, joyfulness, and ease with which a spiritually awakened person lives life. When the Source of such a life is brought into the home or the workplace, others are sure to notice and eventually to ask about it. Then is the optimal time to give witness to the way we have found truth.

Step Twelve also invites us to go beyond the practice of evangelizing through example, however. Having worked through the Steps and discovered how to use them for balance in daily living, we recognize that many people need what we have found, and we cannot simply wait for them to ask us about it. In Alcoholics Anonymous, for example, one is encouraged to make Step Twelve calls and visits — to reach out to active alcoholics and invite them to recovery. Reaching out is true to the spirit of the Bible, where we meet a God who comes looking for us — who is in constant pursuit of the lost sheep who have gone astray. The method and timing for this outreach is something we must discern. The best way is to invite the other to attend a Twelve Step meeting or retreat. But do not discount the power of one-on-one sharing, especially if you can speak about your life and your experiences.

This spirit of outreach is undoubtedly one of the reasons for the success of the Twelve Step movement. From the beginning, Bill W. and Dr. Bob, cofounders of AA, discovered that "you can't give what you don't have, but you can't keep what you don't share." They learned that helping other alcoholics find sobriety helped them stay sober, too. The lesson for all of us is that the spiritual life leads us to know the reality of Love, and this experience grows as we give it away. In the process, we are blessed, and others are brought onto the journey. Only God can work such a miracle!

Daily Living

Step Twelve calls for "practicing these principles in all our affairs." In other words, what we have learned in the Steps must be brought into our daily lives and become a way of life for us. Daily life is not a thing apart from the spiritual journey; the two must become one and the same.

We have discussed many spiritual principles in this book. Which ones do Step Twelve call us to practice?

In concluding this chapter, I will identify four that are foundational for ongoing growth:

1. *Honesty, especially emotional honesty with self, God, and others, is the cornerstone.* Without honesty, a moral life, much less a spiritual life, is not possible.
2. *Awareness, being here-now, resisting useless and negative preoccupation.* Do what you're doing and nothing else.
3. *Surrender, letting go of things you cannot control — in yourself, other people, and the world.* Entrust these to the care of God, and then do what is yours to do in serenity and trust.
4. *Forgiveness, letting go of hurts others have caused you, letting go of self-hatred.* Realize that God has let go of all this and that you cannot really live unless you let go, too. It is God's will that you live this moment awake, and to do this, you must let go of the past.

These four principles, joined with a life of prayer and service in community, will take one all the way on the spiritual journey. Without these four principles, God's work of grace in us will be frustrated. If we work them, however, we maintain the soils of our heart as fertile ground, allowing the seed of grace planted by the Spirit to transform us into the people God has created us to be.

Questions for Reflection

1. How have the Twelve Steps helped you to come to a spiritual awakening?
2. How has the example of another person helped you grow closer to God?
3. How do you try to "carry this message to others"? What have been some of your rewards and failures?
4. Many have said that the Twelve Steps are a way of life. Are you coming to experience this? Explain.

Christian
Twelve Step Groups

I recommend that the group designate a facilitator to assure that the meeting stays focused and follows the suggested format. Two people can share the role of facilitator, rotating the duties from one month to the next.

Each meeting should last about an hour, followed by refreshments and fellowship. A suggested format is described below, with three options for handling the main part of the meeting.

I. Call to Order. (The whole group meets together.) Welcome. Introductions.

II. Opening Prayer. Serenity Prayer. (Recited aloud by entire group.)

God, grant me the serenity to accept the things I cannot change, the courage to change the things I can, and the wisdom to know the difference. Living one day at a time, enjoying one moment at a time. Accepting hardships as the pathway to peace. Taking, as He did, this sinful world as it is, not as I would have it. Trusting that He will make all things right if I surrender to His will; that I may be reasonably happy in this life, and supremely happy with Him forever.

(Reinhold Niebuhr)

III. The Twelve Steps. One or more group members read aloud the Twelve Steps.

IV. The middle section of the meeting may follow one of the following three formats and should be kept to about forty minutes.

A. Step Study Option.
1. In a large-group context, a teaching on how to live one of the steps might be held, followed by open discussion in the large group.
2. Another option is small-group sharing based on focus questions provided by the presenter.

B. Discussion Meeting Option.
1. In a large-group setting, read the gospel for the coming Sunday.
2. Break into groups of four to ten to discuss the following:
   a. What kinds of principles do you hear the gospel emphasizing? How do you relate these to the Twelve Steps?
   b. Which of the Twelve Steps have you been working with lately? How is this affecting your life?
   c. Open discussion: What would you like to hear from

other group members about living the Christian life
or working the Twelve Steps?

   d. Wrap-up: (five minutes). When the facilitator an-
   nounces time for wrap-up, members begin to close
   group by asking, "At this meeting, I have learned
   or relearned...."

C. Book Study Option. Read a chapter of *Twelve Steps to
Spiritual Wholeness* aloud together and discuss the questions at the end of the chapter in groups of four to ten. If
members know in advance that this will be the format,
they will be able to reflect on the questions before the
meeting and come prepared to discuss them.

V. Prayer. In a large-group setting, join hands and say the
Lord's Prayer.

VI. Announcements. Time and place of next meeting, in-
dividuals needing help, and so forth.

VII. Refreshments and Fellowship.

APPENDIX TWO

The Twelve Steps of Alcoholics Anonymous

1. We admitted we were powerless over alcohol — that our lives had become unmanageable.
2. Came to believe that a Power greater than ourselves could restore us to sanity.
3. Made a decision to turn our will and our lives over to the care of God *as we understood Him.*
4. Made a searching and fearless moral inventory of ourselves.
5. Admitted to God, to ourselves and to another human being the exact nature of our wrongs.
6. Were entirely ready to have God remove all these defects of character.
7. Humbly asked Him to remove our shortcomings.
8. Made a list of all persons we had harmed, and became willing to make amends to them all.
9. Made direct amends to such people wherever possible, except when to do so would injure them or others.

10. Continued to take personal inventory and when we were wrong promptly admitted it.
11. Sought through prayer and meditation to improve our conscious contact with God *as we understood Him,* praying only for knowledge of His will for us and the power to carry that out.
12. Having had a spiritual awakening as the result of these Steps, we tried to carry this message to alcoholics, and to practice these principles in all our affairs.

Suggested Reading
on the Twelve Steps

Alcoholics Anonymous. *Twelve Steps and Twelve Traditions.* New York: Alcoholics Anonymous World Services, Inc., 1953.

Friends in Recovery Staff. *The Twelve Steps — A Spiritual Journey: A Working Guide Based on Biblical Teachings.* San Di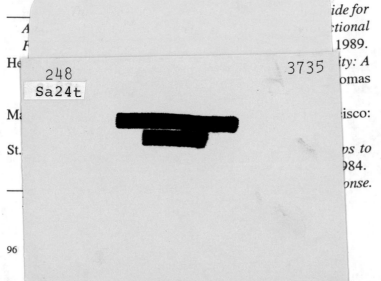

_____ *ide for*
A *:tional*
F 1989.

He *ity: A*
omas

M: *isco:*

St. *ps to*
984.

_____ *onse.*